The Everyday Apostle

Also by Edward F. Garesché
from Sophia Institute Press®:

A Marian Devotional

Edward F. Garesché

The Everyday Apostle

Commonsense Ways
to Draw Others to Christ

SOPHIA INSTITUTE PRESS®
Manchester, New Hampshire

The Everyday Apostle: Commonsense Ways to Draw Others to Christ is an abridged edition of *Your Neighbor and You* (St. Louis: The Queen's Work Press, 1912). This 2002 edition by Sophia Institute Press® contains minor editorial revisions to the original text.

Sophia Institute Press®
Box 5284, Manchester, NH 03108
1-800-888-9344
www.sophiainstitute.com

Imprimi potest: Alexander J. Burrowes, S.J.,
Vice Provincialis Praep. Prov. of Missouri
Nihil obstat: Remigius Lafort, S.T.D., *Censor*
Imprimatur: Joannes Cardinalis Farley, Archbishop of New York

Library of Congress Cataloging-in-Publication Data

Garesché, Edward F. (Edward Francis), 1876-1960.
    The everyday apostle : commonsense ways to draw others to Christ /
    Edward F. Garesché.
        p. cm.
    Abridged ed. of: Your neighbor and you. 1912.
    Includes bibliographical references.
    ISBN 1-928832-49-0 (alk. paper)
    1. Christian life — Catholic authors. 2. Apostolate (Christian
    theology) I. Garesché, Edward F. (Edward Francis), 1876-1960.
    Your neighbor and you. II. Title.
BX2350.3 .G32 2002
248.4′82 — dc21   2001008400

02 03 04 05 06 07 08 09   10 9 8 7 6 5 4 3 2 1

To my father and mother

Contents

Preface

Editor's note: The biblical quotations in the following pages are taken from the Douay-Rheims edition of the Old and New Testaments. Where applicable, quotations have been cross-referenced with the differing names and enumeration in the Revised Standard Version, using the following symbol: (RSV =).

These chapters have for the most part appeared in the pages of the *Messenger of the Sacred Heart*. Some have been published in *America, The Sacred Heart Review, The Magnificat, Extension, Men and Women,* and *The Rosary*. Although written at different times, they group themselves — by design — around one central theme, for they deal with those two greatest of all realities after God Himself: your neighbor and you.

Their appeal is meant to be a wide one; indeed, the thoughts they dwell on are for all earnest and sincere Catholic men and women. Desires often come to all of us to rise to nobler and better ways of living, to make more of our lives both for our neighbor and ourselves. But when, where, and how to begin our efforts often seems difficult and obscure. For religious, there are many manuals of holy living; for the layman, there are comparatively few; fewer still deal with life as it is lived at our present time. These papers are only a partial and feeble effort to supply this want and to suggest to Catholics at least some of the everyday and easy ways in which they may aid both themselves and their fellowmen.

The Everyday Apostle

If something has been sacrificed to emphasis, to interest, and to clearness; if there is a dwelling on the obvious with many repetitions, and a touch of old-fashioned familiarity toward the gentle reader, all these things will be condoned, we trust, in view of the humble and practical purpose of this little book. It was written (a labor of love) in the between-whiles of busy days; and it is meant to be read in like manner — little by little, in quiet moments, or in your weary or your leisure hours.

The Everyday Apostle

The Apostleship
of the Common Man

Carry out God's work
in your everyday life

It is a weakness of our poor human hearts to wish to be uncommon, unusual, or exceptional — distinguished in some way or other from the men around us — and so we shrink from any term that links us all together, all us poor sons and daughters of Adam, on one level of equality. Men would rather be bizarre, extravagant, or even wicked, some of them, than be common, ordinary, and tamely usual.

Many a person finds a cold discouragement in the thought that he comes under the heading of "common Catholics" — that the work to which God has called him is the everyday Apostleship of the Common Man. We grow disheartened, most of us; we are sorely dispirited and listless and lose all hope of doing anything very much worthwhile for God so soon as we remember that we are, after all, only one of the great, uncounted host of ordinary men, of common Christians, of common soldiers of God. If this listlessness, this despair of doing anything truly great and worthy for God's Church, is apt to chill the endeavor of all common Christians who do not feel themselves called to serve God and His Church in the priesthood or the religious life, it is especially apt to discourage and deter the lowly and simple folk among us, the man and woman who feel that their talents, their influence or their opportunities give them no weight with men, and that they are, in the full sense of the term, only very common, obscure, and uninfluential folk indeed.

Yet how wrong and foolish all this is! For are not the common things the most necessary and important? Are battles fought and victories won without the aid of the common soldier? Let us look with God's eyes on our lot, our talents, and our opportunities, and we shall be wonderfully cheered and encouraged — we ordinary men — and heartened to do manfully and well the great work He has set before us, which He will have none do for Him but we ourselves.

"God must love the common people," said shrewd Abraham Lincoln. "He makes so many of them." And in its way, the saying holds a deal of truth. For what God loves in us is not our petty little talents or riches or distinctions, unspeakably small and trivial in His eyes; what He loves in us is our humanity, made to His image and raised by grace to be in a wonderful way His very image indeed!

He loves us as common men, gifted with His grace, plodding through weary ways, toward the glory of our common Heaven! Notice, in connections such as this, how that poor word *common* loses all its low and sorry meanings and becomes fit to describe even the glory of the saints!

God loves us, then — all of us — as common men. Our differences and distinctions, each from each, by which some of us seem to tower mountain-high above the rest, are as nothing to Him, who sees all things as they are. It is our own poor selves, let us say it once again, our body and our soul, and above all, the sanctifying grace that He has given us of His common bounty, that makes us precious in the clear eyes of God. We must realize this very deeply, or we shall never have the courage to do the work God wills. Let us bring it home to ourselves by some further thoughts.

Once there lived around the lake Genesareth, in the obscure land of Palestine, twelve seemingly very ordinary men. There was Simon and Andrew, his brother, who were fishermen. So were John and James, the sons of Zebedee. There was Nathaniel, of Cana in Galilee, an out-of-the-way country place, and Philip and Bartholomew and the rest — all very ordinary men. Last of all, there was Levi, a cursed publican, a pariah among his own people, with whom perhaps none of the rest had ever spoken, for he was beneath even their social level, the lowliest of common men.

Now, as we all know, it was these twelve common men who evangelized the world! How did it happen? We know the story well. Jesus of Nazareth passed by and called them to be His disciples. He taught them His heavenly doctrine. He bade them go abroad over the earth and preach His kingdom to mankind.

Better men than they might well have been pardoned for drawing back in fear; but although they were ordinary men, His grace made them humble, patient, and obedient, and they went forth simply and trustingly and changed the world.

Of course, we other ordinary men and women will straightway object that these Apostles touched and heard the Savior, the Light of the World, that they had their mission from His

very lips, that the Holy Spirit of God descended on them, and
that they had high and superhuman powers of miracles and
prophecy. But so have you heard Christ, from the lips of His
priests, His chosen envoys; so have you touched Him (most
sweetly and efficaciously!) in Holy Communion; so has God
given you a mission to spread His word, if you will only heed.

Your faith is your mission, which must be made known
among all men, among the pagans of this day, as among the
pagans of that earlier time. Your hope is your mission, which
gives you such earnest of a vast reward for your brotherly toil
for other men. Above all, your charity is your mission, which
stirs you to love God and your neighbor with a sincere heart,
diligent to labor and suffer in bringing your neighbor to the
love of God.

And the Holy Spirit? He has been with you from your Bap-
tism, unless you drove Him from you. He came to you in greater
intimacy in Confirmation. He chose you then with a solemn
choice to be a soldier and apostle of Christ.

As for the miracles and the prophecies: these were needful
to the Apostles, because they were to preach a new and hard
doctrine to an incredulous world. But we, Christ's lesser apostles, are to use instead of these extraordinary arguments, the
simple persuasion of good lives, of simple charity, of the light
of holiness and virtue that our deeds are to make to shine in
the eyes of men.

Let us go forth, then, you and I, common men, ordinary
men, what you will, as God made us, with all our limitations,
our faults, and our weaknesses. Let us go forth, honestly and
simply, to the divine and holy work that God has given us to

do in this world. Let us go forth and quietly, and earnestly, and tenderly speak with our brothers and sisters, common men and women like us. They are exceedingly many, and very needy and blind and poor in the goods of life eternal, and we have the light and the doctrine, the wisdom and riches of Christ's true Faith. We have that to give them, for want of which they languish in darkness — and we can so easily give it by our everyday example, our words, and our deeds.

Let us, by our deeds no less than by our words, tell them of that Christ who, being the serene and all-sufficient God, became, as it were, a common man among us out of His eternal tenderness and pity, having compassion on us all, on us common men. Let us tell them that He has come to rescue and redeem our common humanity, to solve our common problems, and to show us the price and value of our lives and all the priceless opportunities that lie around us in the world, around us common men.

Indeed, as we have said before, if we push the meaning of this term *common* a little farther, perhaps we might bring all mankind within its compass and might say that we are all only this, in His vision, the best and the worst of us alike, only common and ordinary men. We may have genius to make a tinkle in the ears of the world, but in His ears, our wit and our wisdom are all very foolish and shallow indeed, the prattle of babies. We may have wealth, station, and power; but in His sight we wither like grass. We may be prelates or princes, wise or holy in men's esteem, but in His eyes, we are but poor, pitiful little ones, common men whom He came to rescue from a common ruin that would have swallowed us all.

The Everyday Apostle

So, each one of us shall be saved by His mercy, not as great men or rich, nor as poor or little, but merely as what we are: common men. It is our humanity that we take with us to Heaven; if we are not saved as common men, vain indeed will have been all the uncommon things we boasted of in this world!

It was this thought that made the great heart of St. Paul groan, in the midst of his labors, "lest perhaps having preached to others, I myself should become a castaway!"[1] The seer, the prophet, the apostle: under the robe of all these Heaven-sent dignities, there lived and breathed, there prayed and suffered, only a common man, solicitous for his soul!

As we are to be saved as common men, so must we serve God; so may we save other men and bring them with us to Heaven. The appeal of our human kindness, sincerity, and love will win them over; our homely and familiar talk will sink conviction into their souls; the power of our everyday example will bring them to believe that Christian goodness is possible, will move them to own that it is sweet and lovely and holy, will make them yearn to bring it into their own hearts and lives. The grasp of our hands will cheer and reassure them; we shall win them, by our common and familiar words and deeds of brotherliness, faith, and love.

Such reflections as these have served to make great men humble, when they considered how small and ordinary they must seem in the eyes of God. But they should have power, too, to stir up and hearten to heroic effort the man who knows

---

[1] 1 Cor. 9:27.

that he is not greatly gifted with power, talent, and influence to aid his fellowmen.

Not one of us, however lowly and undistinguished, who dwells seriously on these thoughts should fail to find in them encouragement and cheer to take up the work God has cut out for him, among the men and women who make up the circle of his little world, to enter boldly on his own special field of apostleship. If we could only bring those great numbers of Catholic men and women, who form the noble ranks of the common faithful, to realize deeply their opportunities and their powers, how soon their valiant efforts could change the face of the earth!

For only think of the numbers, the influence, of all our countless multitudes of plain and simple Catholics throughout the world! They are everywhere; they speak to everyone; everyone is their acquaintance; everyone is their friend. Wherever toilers or feasters or players are gathered together, wherever work is being done or recreations are afoot or men are talking to one another; in car or factory or office or club, the common Catholic is there. He rubs shoulders with all men; he is rich among the rich and poor with the poor, simple with the simple and learned among the learned. In a word, he is, by his very multiplicity and variety and omnipresence, what the great apostle strove ever to be: "all things to all men."[2]

How endless, then, and how various are the opportunities of his apostleship! Where the priest may not enter unsuspected, the common Catholic is already there, a familiar and a friend.

[2] 1 Cor. 9:22.

The Everyday Apostle

His common talk is listened to with interest and without suspicion; his testimony is accepted; his teaching will pass current as the word of a friend. Without suspicion, without prejudice, he can, if it is prudent and tactful, preach the saving truths of his Faith in a thousand places, where the word of a priest of God would be met only with anger, or distrust, or disdain.

If we can only enlist, somehow, the aid of the common man! If we can only awaken in him a sense of his high privileges and noble opportunities, and set him in the way of helping his fellowmen, what great good we shall gain for the Church, and therefore for the world!

Yet, let us say it again in sadness, the great pity is that most men who realize that they come under the category of common Christians, of ordinary Catholics, that they are in no wise distinguished from the great mass of the faithful, either in learning, or influence, or authority, or position, or power of any kind, are apt to be so very easily discouraged and to lose heart for any effort to better the world. They go indeed, only too often, to a sad extreme of what we may call spiritual do-nothingness. Far from exercising any apostleship among their fellowmen, their only ambition seems to be to keep as passive and as quiet as possible in matters of religion and to leave the whole burden of spreading the knowledge of the Faith, of fighting truth's battles and upholding the honor of the Church "to those who are better fit" — by which they commonly mean priests.

Others still, of the ordinary faithful, are bewildered when they are told that they have a mission or an apostleship to this poor, weak, wicked world! What should they do? Where shall they begin? Who will listen to them?

Between these two attitudes of mind, there are a hundred others, all the various shades of discouragement, bewilderment, indifference, and (shall we say it?) laziness, too, which keep our ordinary Catholics from coming forward to take up the labors of this great apostleship.

Now and again you find one or another simple layman who has been touched by God's grace and stirred by some prudent counsel and suggestion to try his hand at spreading the Faith. If such a one is wise, tactful, and persistent, what a great deal he can do! He grows surprised himself at his own accomplishment. He becomes a living proof of what we said in the beginning about the power of the common man. He penetrates where God's priest could never find admittance; he is heard and believed, trusted and followed by men who would resent and suspect the intrusion of any minister of religion in their lives.

But these zealous, enlightened, prudent apostles are still, alas, all too few among our common Catholic men and women. The great majority, with all their great powers unrealized and unused, are waiting, discouraged and obscure, for the suggestion and appeal that might launch them upon their labors for God, for His Church, and for the world.

In conclusion, then, it is to you, dear Catholic reader, whoever or wherever you may be, that these thoughts should have a poignant and urgent appeal. You are one of that chosen people to whom Jesus Christ has given the charge of letting your light shine before men, that they may glorify your Father who is in Heaven.[3] You are one of those to whom St. Peter's words are said, ringing down the ages: "You are a chosen generation, a kingly priesthood, a holy nation, a purchased people: that you may declare His virtues who hath called you out of darkness into His marvelous light."[4]

You, whoever you may be, are one of those everyday apostles to whom is entrusted — for good or for ill — the soul's welfare of scores, perhaps of hundreds and thousands of your fellowmen.

The field of your labors for God lies all around you. It is the world you live in, the men, women, and children you meet every day in familiar interchange, at home, at your work, abroad. Their eyes are upon you. Their ears are listening for your teaching. You cannot help moving, teaching, leading them, either for good or for evil.

Lead a life like the rest of men, follow their foolish ways, dissemble your lofty principles, yield to hate, envy, greed, and lust because "everybody does," and you will quench a great light out of the world. You will be a lesser Judas, a traitor-apostle. You will preach to men, at least in action, that Christ's doctrine is only a lovely theory, His faith an amiable myth, His mission to men a pleasant and impracticable dream. You will quench and smother, so far as in you lies, the flame that should kindle the world!

Be a consistent, wholehearted, faithful Catholic. Speak and act and think and love as your Faith and your conscience bid

[3] Matt. 5:16.
[4] 1 Pet. 2:9.

you, and you will lead them irresistibly toward the truth, toward God and Heaven. Speak to them tactfully and kindly of the Faith that is in you, and your holy example will give your words a weight they cannot resist or gainsay.

The Apostleship
of Speech

☙

Let your conversation
draw others to Christ

The press, mighty and far-reaching as it is, has, we all know, its own peculiar limitations and needs a complement. Many of us cannot write, many lack the time or inclination, and even when it is duly sent forth, the printed page is never quite sure of its audience. This man will not read except for amusement; the other distrusts whatever savors of the supernatural; a third is steeled beforehand against anything that hints of Catholicism or the Church.

But the kindly, spontaneous speech of man to man is easy and common to us all. It murmurs everywhere — in the car, on the street, in offices and homes — kindling its own interest, winning attention, and appealing to every person, in spite of his prejudices and his inclinations. It opens an easy way for that genial interchange of personal opinion, of question and answer, of objection and reply, which clears and recommends as nothing else can, our true beliefs, principles, and points of view.

Of course, no one nowadays would praise mere controversy or polemics. Heaven forbid! That odious and ugly wrangling over sacred truths, which only adds stubbornness to each man's conviction, is happily out of mode. But we are in danger of going to the other extreme and following the indifferentism of the age so far that we carefully avoid every mention of sacred things.

We are sometimes guilty of his cruel kindness and complaisance even toward our nearest and dearest friends. Cruel we must call it, because we are keeping from them, by our silence, the very truths and principles that we hold as our dearest and most precious possession in this world. If a readiness to share money, influence, and opportunities is looked for between friends, how much more should there be a frank and willing communication of those eternal truths which enrich and ennoble a man's immortal soul. Yet, if we treated one another in matters of dollars and cents as we do in issues of the soul's salvation, some of us would have few friends left in the world.

Once, in the murmur and clatter of a crowded streetcar, an angry voice rose over the hum of city noises: "You knew the firm was going under," it shouted in ungovernable fury, "and you let me go ahead with the deal!" A moment's pause followed, in which we might imagine a murmured reply. "You knew I was in for losing, and you were on the right side, and you didn't say a word!" cried the voice again. "You cur! That may be your idea of friendship, but it isn't mine. Don't talk to me again!"

The angry man was right. That was no true friend who let him stake his money on a rotten venture and never said a word. Heaven grant that our own friends may not have cause to hurl a like reproach at us on the Judgment Day!

Let your conversation draw others to Christ

I remember still the regretful pathos with which a dear old gentleman, who in the thoughtlessness of youth had entered into associations that kept him from his religious duties, told me of the strange silence that everyone kept toward him on that one subject of which he had most need to hear. "There was So-and-so," said he, "a good Catholic, and a firm friend of mine, but he never said the word. And there was Fr. N. Many a time I laughed and chatted with him, but he never said the word. And there's X, and Y, and Z. . . . Ah," the old man would wish, "and now that I'm back in the Church of God, it seems to me I've lost most of my life!" All for want of the word!

None of us can plead a lack of such occasions. Many a Catholic nowadays is almost solitary in a circle of unbelieving associates. Is silence friendly, then?

The man who drops into a seat beside you and wishes you a cheery good morning may be starved and stinted of all knowledge of things divine. More than possibly, as things stand now in the United States, he has never said a childish prayer by his mother's knee; never learned to reverence the Sacred Name; never heard, at home or at school, the saving truths of Christ; never once been brought face-to-face with the stupendous truths that there is an infinite God, and that man has an immortal soul. It is not malice with him, this denseness to sacred truth. It is ignorance; it is preoccupation.

This is a distracted age. We live fast; we notice only what is thrust upon us. All that a person has heard of God's Holy Name may have been (dreadful thought) when it was used in blasphemy, or as the nice ornament of some well-turned phrase, or, at best, as a vague symbol of nature or humankind, lacking personality and dim of definition. Religion to this man may be only the queer fancy some men have to while away a Sunday morning. That God is a person, even as he is; that the soul has ages of endless life before it; that the world is only a trying-out place for the brightest or darkest hereafter; that there is a Hell, the blaze of the anger of God, and a Heaven, the smile of His tenderness; that every man and woman is sacred, is of God's own kindred; that what seems blind chance is only a bit, ill-seen, of the vast schemes of Infinite Prevision — what does he know, what has he ever dreamed, of all these things?

But you are his friend. He will listen to you, if you are ready to offer a kindly explanation. He is interested, after all, in most things human, in your affairs particularly.

What a revelation to his ignorance, and what a stimulus from his dangerous preoccupation with merely earthly and temporal things, if you were sometimes to take occasion from current themes to explain those lovely and satisfying doctrines of the Church, which please and thrill by their beauty and saneness even where faith does not enter in and beget acceptance of their truth!

If it were golf you were interested in, or stocks, or futures, or horses, or a new brand of goods, or a coming marriage, it would go hard, but he would have to listen all the way downtown — and right cheerfully. Well, try him sometimes, with kindly tact and opportunely, on some Catholic theme.

"But how, in the name of goodness," I seem to hear someone cry out sadly, "am I to be ready to give good explanations on Catholic subjects?"

Let your conversation draw others to Christ

A proper question, and one that calls for a whole treatise by itself. But we can condense after the manner of the testy gentleman who cried out in answer to a similar inquiry: "God bless you, sir! Why not go and read?"

Naturally, to be a proper Catholic, we must glance now and then at Catholic papers and have some acquaintance with Catholic magazines and books. Surely we Catholics can all endure to become prompt and ready with the warm and human, yet divine and heavenly, truths and principles of Christ.

Wrong-headed folk, with flimsy theories, have often a dreadful gift of voluble exposition, which puts us children of the light to shame. In season and out of season, they din away at their pet theory, until, by mere repetition, they wear it a place in men's thoughts, or even a standing in their esteem. We must not imitate their fanatical excesses — indeed, there is little danger as things go with us now; but the temper of the times is such that even the truth cannot dispense with some of this emphasis of repetition and ready reply. The age is crowded with clamoring teachers; if even truth is silent, it will be unregarded as well. On the other hand, by kindly explanation, timely comment, and friendly expostulation and reply, our beliefs and views are sure to gain a hearing, and a hearing is all that Catholic truth need ask.

Look on this picture: our friend Dick has a fearfully keen nose for controversy. His type, I own, is somewhat rare these days. Give him but a little opening, and he will argue away for hours, with the slightest encouragement — nay, in spite of the most evident distaste and disgust on the part of his unwilling victim. Dick means well, to be sure (his selfishness is half unconscious). He knows a great deal, his speech is fluent and sincere; he lacks only the heavenly gift of tact and opportuneness, but lacking this, his acrid fluency has made many a helpless fellow sore on religion and savage against pious talk for all afterdays.

Tom, on the other hand, and his name is many, runs quite to the other extreme. He is the most discreet fellow in the world and sheers off from questions of belief and principles like a timid hare at the hunter's halloo! He seldom breathes a word that can benefit anyone. His talk is remote from religious issues, and most of his friends scarcely know whether he is a Catholic or a fellow of Huxley or of the German visionaries. He breaks a commandment. His light never shines at all!

Harry, on the other hand — God bless him! — holds the difficult mean. When he speaks of religious matters, he does it in as easy, interested a way as when he talks politics or business. His mind runs naturally on the theme, and his interest carries you with him. He knows, and he thinks on what he knows, and remembers it readily and in opportune connections. There is neither false shame nor harsh self-assertiveness in his tone. You see earnest-faced men listening to his quiet explanations with a sort of steady wonder. And when he pauses, you notice that they sink back and murmur: "By Jove! That sounds sensible. I never could understand just what you Catholics thought on that point before." Ah, if there were only more Harrys now among us!

The Apostleship
of Service

❧

Accept every opportunity
to do good

I once knew an amiable old gentleman — not so very old either, but in that mellow way of life in which a person's little ways are set forevermore — who had a gift for many useful things. He could make you anything you liked in wood, and make it beautifully, with a trim, old-fashioned completeness few modern carvers or joiners can attain. He could make relishes — old-world relishes — full of piquant savors that made simple fare a feast for kings. He could mend precious broken things — old china or trinkets — that you mourned over, so that their last state was prettier than the first. There was no end to the neat and useful things this much-accomplished man could do.

"What a convenient person to have around you," you will straightway think to yourself. So, to be sure, he was. Yet the full comfort and usefulness of his varied talents was hindered a bit by a single oddity he had. Whenever you approached him, as people often did, to ask the exercise of one of his varied talents, he would give you a rueful glance and, screwing up his forehead in regret, would answer mournfully, "I'd gladly fix it for you, so gladly, but, you know, I'm not *rigged* to do it." That was the haunting shadow that stalked his path. He was never rigged!

Let us hasten to add that it was not laziness in him — not in the least. Nor was it a cheap excuse, nor any unwillingness to oblige and serve you that made him say it. He was the most serviceable of men and as full of kindness as summer is of sunshine.

It was a real and obstinate difficulty he always saw, crouching like a lion in his way. He was not rigged to do it. Perhaps it was a tool that he must absolutely have to polish off his work, and which, he knew for certain, was nowhere in the county. Perhaps it was some delicate ingredient, if you spoke of relishes, without which his best recipe was a mere mess and silly failure, and which didn't grow, he was sure, anywhere this side of salt water. Perhaps — oh, there were any number of perhapses, but the gist of them all was this: he simply wasn't rigged to do it!

Of course, with his kind heart, it was not so hard to get him over this mountainous objection. And once he had set his mind to do the thing you asked, rigged or not rigged, his ingenuity was a match for anything. He could use tools out of all measure of their common purpose and make a penknife do for any tool. He could torture allspice and onions until they breathed of tarragon and make a homely kitchen garden yield all the savors of Gascony and Spain. But despite these various resources of his native genius, that thought forever haunted him like an obsession and held his hand from any trial of skill; that sad refrain was ever in his ears: "I'm not rigged to do it."

Accept every opportunity to do good

How I would like, if morals were not so tedious, to cut a sheaf of serviceable comparisons from the amiable eccentricity of that good man I knew! You and I, my dear and patient reader, have given the same excuse, many a time, to save the doing of some golden deed. Do you remember, when the good thought came to you — of what? — some deed of mercy and kindness, not easy, perhaps, to do, but rich in promise of results. It came like an inspiration. Who knows? Perhaps it was truly a message from the Father of lights, bidding you to help your brother. You were moved to do it generously; you planned the ways and means. Then came chill calculation, with its selfish breath, and blew cold on your generous fervor. You said, in effect at least, "I'm not rigged to do it. If I had more time, if I had more talents, if I were in a position to do the thing as it should be done, if I were the proper person, if circumstances were other than they are, if this, if that — ah, then, then I would do it gladly, nobly, effectively. But now, alas, I'm not rigged." So the inspiration faded; the little voice within you faltered and was still; the opportunity escaped you. That credit stands forever blank for you on the great ledgers of the Chancery of Heaven.

Or again, it was some work of zeal that called upon us. Perhaps we were asked to bear our share in aiding some noble charity. Perhaps it was our personal effort that was wanted to help a good cause. How many chances for unselfish effort have come to our doors and knocked, perhaps tapped only timidly, perhaps rapped long and loud! And we, opening a little chink, lest they should rush in on us unawares and spoil our calm seclusion, have answered through the cranny, "Pray, excuse me;

The Everyday Apostle

I'm not rigged. To tell the truth, I can't see my way to aid you. Another time, maybe, when this and that and the other are off my hands. But now, I really haven't got the time or the money. I'm not rigged to do it. I pray you, go away; importunate or timid pleader, hold me excused."

And the good deed went on to the door of a neighbor, far, far less rigged, perhaps, than we, and it was welcomed and entered in and blessed the dwelling. But our opportunity is passed away.

Did you smile, dear reader, when you thought of the queer persuasion of yonder old friend of mine, that he was never "rigged" to exercise his various crafts and talents? So do the angels smile at us for so often thinking that we are not rigged to do the good that comes to seek us. My friend's ingenuity and deftness were far more than a match for any ordinary awkwardness of tools or stuff; he was always "rigged" by his own natural genius to do whatever he had a mind to. So could we accomplish many a worthy deed we balk at now, if only we were content to use the homely means that lie about us and within us.

Now, gentle reader, descend from generalities and look about you a bit, and see how many good works lie ready to your hand. Will you say, "I'm not rigged to do them"?

There are your own home-folk, the people of your intimate acquaintance. Have you not had many a thought of them; of good words that you might speak to them, to cheer them and guide them along better ways; of kind encouragement and sympathy that you could offer, to help them through dangerous passes or hearten them along noble paths? Could you not, many a time, instruct or admonish or console them, as each one needs? If you say, "I'm not prepared," what does that mean? Merely that you are not perfect, that you might be better fit. Who among mortals could not say the same with regard to any worthy undertaking whatever? Any man or woman among us, with prudence and right feeling, can give some worthy aid to his own people, in his own circle of friends.

Then there is the wider sphere of your acquaintances. We can give only the vaguest outlines here, which everyone must sketch in for himself. Have we not some friends who need a word of kindly instruction in matters of religious practice and belief? Could we not say the word and aid them on toward Heaven? "I'm not ready," "I don't know enough myself," "I hesitate to intrude, with my very scanty qualifications" — in a word, "I'm not rigged to do it," so God's work must go undone.

See how we could widen the application of this little instance until it helped us to account for half the ignorance, the folly, and the sin that blight the earth. The ignorant are ignorant still; the foolish and the sinful are unadmonished, because the men and women who might tactfully and lovingly step in and remedy the evil "are not prepared," "do not feel equal to the task," "are not quite fit just now." They're not rigged to do it!

Does God mean us to act so, do you think? Will He take this monotonous excuse of ours for leaving His work so sadly undone and for failing so mournfully to help our sisters and brothers toward His knowledge and His service and His love? For — here is a very serious thought indeed — we sometimes seem to throw the blame on God with this sorry excuse of ours.

The Everyday Apostle

He gives to us these duties, these opportunities, these suggestions of His grace — to us and to no others, no angel and no saint. He gives them to us as we are, not as we might, or could, or would, or should have been. It is to us with our imperfections, our shortcomings, our insufficiencies, our ignorance, and our little worth that He has given in charge the welfare of our brother's soul, perhaps even his soul's salvation. For the one word that he will take may be one that only we could give him. He may be waiting for our word of counsel, teaching, or admonition. We, and we only, may have the key to fit the rusty wards of his poor heart. How sad if we should hold back and fail to say the word, because, forsooth, we're "not rigged."

We may say as much about the many other avenues of effort on behalf of God, of the Church, of Catholic charities, which stretch away before each Catholic's feet. If you have leisure, there are the many works of social charity: helping the poor, housing the homeless child, teaching the ignorant, visiting the prisoner, nursing the sick, comforting the sorrowful and the unhappy — all, in a word, of the various and precious works that we call corporal works of mercy. Then there are the spiritual works of mercy, too.[5] Surely all of us are fit and equal and able for some of these.

---

[5] The corporal works of mercy are to feed the hungry; to give drink to the thirsty; to clothe the naked; to shelter the homeless; to visit the sick; to ransom the captive; and to bury the dead. The spiritual works of mercy are to instruct the ignorant; to counsel the doubtful; to admonish sinners; to bear wrongs patiently; to forgive offenses willingly; to comfort the afflicted; and to pray for the living and the dead.

Accept every opportunity to do good

Let us go back again to our kindly old friend of the beginning and from his memory draw a happy omen. He, you will remember, although he was always haunted by that dark apprehension of not being rigged to do it, got over it bravely at a few words of affectionate persuasion and turned his skillful hand right manfully to the work he was besought to do. Are not you and I, dear reader, equally good-natured, and will we not, in our weightier tasks of Christian love and charity, copy his hearty compliance, no less than we have copied his quaint excuse? When hereafter a wise and prudent and fruitful thought of doing some good work for God or our neighbor pops into our head, we shall say to ourselves right manfully, not hearing our lower self's denial, "Now, do be good and set to work at it, and don't be offering that tiresome old excuse again: 'Really, you know, I'd like to, but I'm not just rigged to do it.' "

*The Apostleship
of the Home*

*Make your home
a place of holiness*

To love and do good to one another is, after all, a very great part of what we are to accomplish here in this world. And to do ourselves justice, we are usually willing enough to help and benefit our neighbor, if only we see a practicable and present way. Half of those who do next to nothing for others act so because they think of nothing to do. But tell us what is to be done and how to do it, and you shall see some hearty workers indeed.

We have said something already about the Apostleship of Speech — that of frank, kindly, and familiar speech on Catholic subjects and Catholic views and beliefs, with those who come within our everyday circle of influence and appeal. We are all constantly talking to one another, discussing, inquiring, replying, and exchanging opinions and ideas. And so, we said, to become at once a real apostle — that is to say, a messenger, a herald of Catholic ethics and Faith — any one of us needs only to throw into his daily talk some genial, honest, interesting words of Catholic truth.

Now let us descend a little into some of the special forms that this Apostleship of Speech may assume and some of the special opportunities it may offer us. It would be good to begin, where charity does in the proverb, right at home. Fathers and mothers, big brothers and big sisters, I wonder how many of us realize the power we are constantly using for good or ill: the influence of our daily speech at home.

We boast sometimes that *home* is one of the most tender and meaningful words in our English tongue. We declare that many other languages have no real equivalent to convey all the wealth and warmth of loving thought and memory, of kindly, generous feeling that stirs in us at this holy word *home*. To have a happy home is, we rightly think, an unspeakable blessing. To lack a home, for man or woman or child, is a capital and dire misfortune. "A man's home," according to the old English saying that we have made our own, "is his castle," his secure retreat, a kingdom of comfort and of cheer, a little stronghold of affection and interest and kindly sympathy against the rude buffets of this selfish, unfeeling world.

We know, too, when we reflect on the matter, that home is a little commonwealth, where each one has his part to play for the well-being of the whole. Mother and father have, to be sure, a paramount influence; but everyone down to the youngest child has his share in making or unmaking the peacefulness and holiness of home.

In what way is this influence most often and most effectively exerted? To be sure, by our daily and common speech! What is hastily said at breakfast, or slips from us as we pass through the house, or is discussed at the family dinner or chatted about around the evening lamp, or mooted in the parlor — this perhaps most of all, makes or mars the peace and happiness and holiness of our home. For in these chance re-marks, these off-hand conversations and familiar, cozy talks, we throw off countless little hints and coruscations, so to speak, of our most inward and intimate selves. We reveal our sudden thoughts and impulses; we show our desires, our prin-ciples, our aims — all, whether it be good or ill, that we have been cherishing and fostering and brooding over for years and years. These things leap out, sometimes in a tiny sentence, sometimes in a single word like little sparks of goodness or of wickedness, and kindle fires of good or evil in our hearers' inmost hearts. The doors and windows of their hearts are all thrown open in the summer air of trustfulness and love, and our flying words blow in easily for weal or woe.

And this goes on, not for an hour or a day, but for all the long months and years of the familiar interchange of home. No wonder we influence one another by our daily speech of words and actions; for actions, too, are a sort of speech and often carry our meaning much better and more easily than words do.

Parents sometimes feel deeply distressed when they see, growing in their tender children, the lineaments of their own shortcomings and sins. They put on a very serious expression and take Tom or Mary aside to warn him or her earnestly against letting that evil habit gain on him or her. Do they hope that one official warning so ceremoniously given will stand for a moment against the long, quiet talk and action of so many years? "Don't, for Heaven's sake," they say, "get into that ugly way of criticizing people!" But has not the lad heard you for years dwelling on the faults of your friends? Can one brief gust of studied sermonizing avail to sweep away that heavy, brooding cloud of innumerable daily acts and words?

It is worthwhile, then — very, very much worthwhile — to give some care and thought to how we may carry on this Apostleship of the Home. And this should weigh on us all the more because of the circumstance that we must all be either apostles or betrayers there. Abroad, we can fight shy of company and keep pretty much to ourselves, not doing anyone very much good or harm. But it is not so at home. Here we must all be constantly taking sides and influencing our little sphere for good or ill. Talk we must, act we must in the presence of everyone; and not to talk and act properly and well and in a holy way is to talk and act badly, doing our share to mar the sanctity of our home.

Of course, no one will here understand me to mean to commend anything like a sanctimonious way of acting or a forcedly religious style of talk. The only good purpose that these would serve at home would be to start some merry laughter that would bring us to our senses again. But I do most heartily mean that we should particularly and earnestly try always to speak and to act worthily and in a holy way among our own people, by our own fireside.

First, there are things we should not speak of at all. Here we might mention a very host of harmful and ugly subjects that too often, alas, creep into our talk to poison the quiet air of home. The bitter and open word of slander and rash judgment we need not pause to censure, but there is a subtler way of hurting our neighbor by little sneers, discreditable anecdotes, left-handed compliments, which begin, "So-and-so is a good fellow; I always liked the chap, but — " and here follows an unkindly stab. There is a way of speaking of our pastor, our bishop, and whatnot, which some good folk fall into from very thoughtlessness, but which sadly hurts the holiness of home. You know quite well that Father X is a good, fervent man. But he has his faults (as who has not?), and you make free to point them out quite emphatically, over the roast.

"Who is the worse, pray, for that? The grown-ups will understand, and the children don't take any harm!"

Are you so sure that they will understand? Has not a light word of disparagement, carelessly spoken, sometimes tarnished your respect and esteem for a friend?

Again, there is little Tom or Jerry, who listens with wide eyes to everything Papa or Mama or big brother is saying. Can he make excuses or allowances? No, but he can comprehend quite well that, after all, there is something wrong with Father X, to whom the good Sisters always tell him to be so respectful. Do you remember when you were young yourself and made your first discoveries as to the faults of your youthful heroes? How long the memory of such disillusionments remains!

It is a pitiful thing to see the atmosphere of the world creep in and taint the holiness of home. To be forever praising men whose only claim to praise is that they have succeeded in getting name and fame, or lands and gold is pitiful in us travelers toward the Eternal Sunrise; but it is a crime to let the little ones hear us singing our psalms to mammon day after day, as though worldly fortune were the last end of man. Will not they, too, become little idolaters and give incense to the god of gold? Do we not sometimes forget that what we most praise will be what our sons and daughters will very likely most desire in the days to be?

We have dwelled on our duties to children especially, because they are most impressionable and confiding, and will catch most readily the trend and color of their elders' thought. They listen most when we least suspect it and are more interested sometimes in what we say to each other than in what we speak directly to them. But we have a duty to the grown-ups no less. Who can dwell in an atmosphere of pure and worthy speech and not be the better for it? Who can hear unworthy words for long and not run a risk of being himself defiled?

A meaner sort of conversation still is the foolish cackling of the snob. Society and exclusiveness, and the delicate and senseless distinctions between Mr. and Mrs. Tweedledum and the Tweedledees are not fit subjects for the family circle, where should breathe honesty, simplicity, and peace. To worship gold and lands is bad enough in all conscience, but it is hardly so base as to worship social distinctions, airy nothings, too often founded on no solid reasons whatever.

"But what are we to talk of?" An easy answer would be to borrow the words of St. Paul that he wrote to the Philippians in a somewhat different meaning indeed, but which come in very aptly here: "Whatsoever things are true, whatsoever modest, whatsoever just, whatsoever holy, whatsoever lovely, whatsoever of good fame, if there be any virtue, if any praise of discipline, think on these things"[6] and speak of them in the kind commerce of family talk.

[6] Phil. 4:8.

Make your home a place of holiness

Let us descend a bit more into particulars. To put it all in a nutshell, we would like to have more really Catholic talk at Catholic firesides. By Catholic, I do not mean parish talk or church talk, still less talk merely about Catholic men and women, but talk that is concerned with subjects of truly Catholic interest and inspired with Catholic feelings and Catholic thought.

Like it or not, we Catholics are a people apart. We have our own spiritual color, our own characteristics, our own proper beliefs, viewpoints, and principles. Whatever savors of these should be not only sacred to us, but interesting also, and should make some matter of our daily speech. We should know at least the current history of Catholic interests, as a good citizen knows the current history of his native land. A Catholic who does not care to speak of Catholic matters is a far worse anomaly than an American who knows and cares nothing for American interests and affairs. In this regard, we fear, the talk of our Catholic homes is far too colorless.

Mothers and fathers, big sisters and big brothers, do the little ones at home gather from your daily speech that deep loyalty and intelligent interest, that steadfast earnestness and wide-awake zeal with respect to things Catholic, which you would wish them to acquire now in the soft, impressionable days of youth?

We might here mention a whole host of subjects on which Catholic folk should sometimes think and speak at home, but we would have to vary it a bit to suit every reader, for we are not all of equal wit, nor have we all the same interests or the same cares or surroundings. But take up some good Catholic paper and glance with interest at the news it brings of Catholic affairs and doings in this and in other lands. We find there communications from the Holy See to the faithful of Christendom, tidings of Catholic enterprise in charitable and social work, in politics, letters, and art, word of the Church's missionaries, news of her religious orders and congregations, the plans and doings of her layfolk, a thousand and one items of Catholic bearing and significance that Catholic readers should be glad to see.

Truly, to most of us, a greater interest in Catholic papers would give a finer, fuller flow of Catholic speech and Catholic thought. Does not the secular press feed our minds with most of the matter for our casual talk? If we would only read more Catholic books and let the Catholic papers give us more food for thought, our lips would blossom easily enough into worthy and Catholic speech abroad and at home.

I think I hear a strong cry of protest: "Why, to do all this, we would have to begin and educate ourselves all over again!" A very wise observation! Perhaps we should. But is it not worthwhile, for the sake of the holiness and happiness of our own home circle, to learn all over again, if need be, the ways and topics of Catholic speech?

It may need some effort and watchfulness. At first, we may often have to repress the rising word or discipline the frivolous thought, but patience, courage! Every effort means an easier victory next time. And when we have thoroughly reformed and disciplined our speech according to the sane and blessed lines of Catholic principles, we shall, at the same time, have formed our minds and souls nearer to the high ideal of Christian virtue. For, "if any man offend not in word, the same is a perfect man."[7]

When we have learned to speak as we should, to bear our part bravely, kindly, and tactfully in making pure and holy the atmosphere of our homes, we shall indeed have become true apostles, mighty influences for good on all around us. We shall have learned to practice one of the noblest works that is given to man in this world: the work of doing good to others.

[7] James 3:2.

The Apostleship
of Encouragement

Inspire others
with courage and cheer

New Year's Day, following as it does on the Christmas season, finds our hearts open and warm for all good thoughts and resolves of Christian charity. Christmas, above all the feast of love, has filled us so full of kindliness and goodwill that we look for some ready way of showing our neighbor our friendliness and good feeling. Well, there is one way at our hand that is easy, practical, and fruitful: the Apostleship of Encouragement.

We mortals are glad enough ourselves for any bit of helpful, honest encouragement that comes our way, and we like to have everyone hearten us and cheer us on. As to heartening other folk, and cheering them on, that's another matter. We don't see our way to do it tactfully, or we think they might not value our encouragement if it were given, or it might seem an intrusion, or perhaps it never even enters our heads that they stand in need of any help or cheer from us at all.

These are, alas, the common attitudes of mind toward this important matter of lending hope and countenance to other men; these are the reasons why there is too little of this great good in the world.

The Everyday Apostle

If you go back a bit in your experience, and grow meditative about yourself and the people you have known, you will very shortly realize, I think, that you and they have suffered a great deal at certain times in your life from mere, downright discouragement. You may not have been quite conscious at the time of what it was that leaded down your feet or lay like a weight above your heart. You were young, perhaps, and great designs had been forming in your fervid mind of doing worthy deeds and greatly helping on your fellowmen. Possibly your dreams had not much weight and workaday substance to them, but they were evidence of a good will and a lofty purpose — precious things which, when well directed, avail to uplift and purify the world.

But there came a day, perhaps it was after you had tried some too-ambitious flight and fallen rudely, when your great resolves suddenly faltered and flagged. You woke to a sorrowful and half-despairing realization of your own scant equipment for anything really noble and great. You found out the height and the distance of those delectable mountains that had before seemed so easy and so near. And so, seeing no way before you, you bitterly cursed the mirage that had led you into this desert of discouragement, and perhaps you turned your back in sullen disillusionment on all the heroic aspirations and settled down to lead a humdrum life of easy mediocrity, like the greater part of the unheroic world.

Oh, if there had been someone there, some wise and patient and tender heart who could have rallied and reassured you and tided you over this first bitter stroke of withering discouragement! If someone had only been there to remind you that the greatest of men often failed miserably in the beginning and that battles are won only with many bruises and blows! All you required was a little cheerful encouragement, a little elasticity of spirit, and there would have been a new start with better plans and securer guidance along the upward grade. But, alas, no one spoke to any purpose; no one vouchsafed the tiny word of wise encouragement and cheer that you needed to help you over that perilous and critical pass, and so you are what you are, instead of being the noble thing you had meant and hoped and planned to be.

This manner of tragedy is very common in men's lives. Sometimes it is a purpose and effort toward merely temporal honor and service that faints and fails for want of due encouragement. How many a lad who had hoped to be a doughty soldier or a mighty statesman has given up and meekly gone to keeping dusty ledgers, because he found no help in his necessity when his soul was sick and weary for the encouragement of a friend!

Over these merely temporal losses and calamities we need not grieve so much. Sometimes they are not really calamities or losses at all, for they turn a man's eyes from the things of time and set him gazing toward eternity. It is the spiritual and eternal losses we must deplore, and how many of these, how very many indeed, come from a lack of due encouragement!

"We live by admiration, hope, and love," cries Wordsworth in a famous poem, and, to be sure, a great part of our vigor, earnestness, and courage in entering on nobler lives and living up to better resolutions comes from the warm, bright hopes we cherish, and our glowing anticipations of success to be. This is all natural and proper and good. It is true that God made us and it is true, too, that intelligent beings, who act for an end, must cheer themselves and be cheered on past the trials and miseries that wait like lions in the way. Holy contemplatives have even loved to think that the angel who came to comfort our Lord in His agony was sent to bring vividly before His human soul the immense and everlasting joy and glory He was to win by His depths of suffering and humiliation. If this is true, as they have lovingly imagined, if He, the All-sufficient, the All-strong, vouchsafed to let a creature of His will minister to Him, and encourage and console Him, is it any wonder that we, who are pitifully weak and dependent, should sometimes need the cheer and encouragement of our fellowmen to help us on through our small agonies?

Our neighbor's need in his discouragement is, then, it is clear, our own golden opportunity. It opens to us an easy and a glorious apostleship that the simplest and the lowliest of us all may practice very effectively, and which, tactfully and lovingly pursued, will make us true ministering angels to our fellowmen. How thick the opportunities for this blessed apostleship lie round about us all!

First, let us look around us in our own homes, at our own firesides, and see whether some precious occasions for it are not waiting ready to our hand. It may be, for instance, that we have long been trying to influence for good some brother or sister of ours, some near relative or intimate friend.

Perhaps we may fancy to ourselves that we have done everything that flesh and blood can do, to work out our beneficent designs. We have suggested, advised, exhorted, admonished, even scolded, been friendly and severe by turns, but all to no avail. We have tried the direct ways and the roundabout ways, have used ingenuity and bluntness and finesse and subtlety and persuasion, all the loving means and all the hard ones, but still to no avail!

Now let us ask ourselves one most weighty question more: Have we ever tried true and genuine encouragement? To get anyone to make a real effort toward bettering himself, is it not clear that one of the very first requisites is to get him to believe strongly and hope vividly that he can somehow be a better man? This seems a truism, perhaps, but it is often overlooked by sage admonitors. We are too likely to forget, in our superior way, that it is mere downright discouragement and dispiritedness about themselves and their own possibilities of reform which keep many, many poor sinners groveling in their sin. Get a man into a hopeful, eager spirit with himself, keen and sanguine about his own chances of improvement, and you will have given him an immense lift along the paths of righteousness and perfection.

Try once more, then, with these friends of yours, and try this time with the gentle, irresistible means of cordial and tactful encouragement. Cordial and tactful — we may well dwell a while on these two words, for they hold in themselves the essence of true encouraging. Encouragement must be cordial, full of heart. It must spring from no other wish, desire, or impulse than genuine love. Love — unselfish, Christian, patient, generous love — must be its wellspring, its motive and inspiration. Then it will not intrude or offend or defeat its own purpose by ill-concealed arrogance or assumed superiority. It will not wound instead of healing, or weary instead of giving cheer. Second, it must be tactful; not intrusive, or ill-timed or insistent, or self-important or importunate, all of which spring from, and smell of, the musty soil of selfishness.

Now that we are speaking of the things that encouragement does not mean, let us put in just one more word of caution. Encouragement does not mean flattery or insincere approval, or even what is generally known as praise. To praise a man to his face, even to flatter him, is indeed a sort of encouragement, but it is too often not a good sort at all. It is a great deal like those narcotic stimulants that can indeed heighten the heart and screw up the courage for a while, but soon fail and leave a sense of weariness and languor and a fiercer craving for more of the same unhealthy stimulus.

The encouragement we speak of is sensible, homely and moderate, sincere and true, and therefore effective and enduring. If it praises, it praises modestly and truly, choosing to praise the deed rather than the man who does it, not drawing invidious comparisons. It consists in heartening our brother, bringing him with word and deed to the true and healthy optimism that is patient of toil and failure, because by God's help it trusts in victory at the end.

Life as God sees it is always encouraging — a very field of glorious opportunities — and therefore true Christian encouragement is making the disheartened and weary see the world through the ever-cheerful eyes of its Creator and Lord.

"But if we have to be so careful and circumspect about it, it might be a great deal better not to try to encourage other folks at all!" Oh, no, dear interlocutor, it is always better to try! To twist a bit the saying of St. Francis de Sales,[8] it is better by far to encourage with imperfection than not to encourage at all.

With goodwill and a little prudent thinking about what we have done, we shall soon come to have some skill in this noble art of encouragement. What a day that will be, when, at our poor words and looks, we see cheeks flush and eyes brighten with noble energy and courage, where there was before only dull downheartedness and a sort of gloomy half-despair!

If we think that we are not any way fitted to exercise this great apostleship, we should make it a subject of our prayers to God and beg Him to give us the heart and the tact and the will to carry the work along all through our lives. For in all the range of fruitful apostleships, there are few more blessed than this.

It would be pleasant to descend to many details and reflect awhile on some particular occasions for this Apostleship of Encouragement, which come in the way of nearly all of us sometime or other during our lives.

There are the young folk, who seem so abundantly blessed already with life, spirits, and hope that many an elderly man or woman thinks sighingly that they at least are in very little need of encouragement. But it is not true. It is the young who need encouragement perhaps most of all, for they are new to themselves and to the world. They have no memories of deeds well done to cheer and hearten them and make them believe a little in their own capacity and powers. They have no settled station and footing among men to give them strength. They

---

[8] St. Francis de Sales (1567-1622), Bishop of Geneva.

need some kindly voice, some friendly eye to reassure and stir them to confidence and hope. A word of encouragement, a little word of appreciation, then, at the critical time in their young fortunes may have a world of meaning and value in their eyes, may make them your debtors for life and enshrine you in their loving memories through all the changes of afteryears.

Have the old no need of encouragement? Be sure they have! Everyone who is plodding along through this world has. It is true that the discouragements of the old are likely to be quite different from those that chill and depress the mercurial heart of youth. The old suffer from weariness, disillusionment, and regret. They can no longer stir themselves to fresh endeavors and new virtues and holiness, by thinking of the years to be, for with them there are no years to be. All their long days are spread behind them! And they look back on past years with uneasiness and pain. The opportunities they wasted, the good deeds they have left undone, and the evil for which they have never atoned rise up and haunt them now, so that they, too, like the young (although for different reasons), often stand sorely in need of encouragement and cheer.

The middle-aged stand on the great divide of life, facing the westering sun, midway betwixt youth and old age, and the discouragement of both those times of life assails them by turns, and so they are often in need of some cheer and heartening, too.

To put it all in a word, most of the world about us — and particularly when it comes to a question of earnest and exceptional efforts toward greater holiness and virtue — is plodding along in a more or less chronic state of mild discouragement. Many a careless-seeming and loose-living man is really deeply concerned in his own heart about his spiritual welfare and is anxious, in a vague and indefinite sort of way, to be a better fellow and rise out of his sin. What keeps him back from making some definite effort to improve is a despondent feeling that all he can do will be of small avail. Religion seems to him a somber thing, breathing only punishment and gloom. To show him the cheerful and consoling side of Christ's sweet message is to lift him up and urge him on most efficaciously to better things.

Let us set ourselves, then, steadfastly, prudently, and tenderly to take up this holy apostleship of cheering on our fellowmen in the ways of virtuous effort. Let us join the ranks of those noble hearts — alas, too few — whose minds are forever busy in conjuring up and putting to the test ingenious and tender ways to help and cheer along their neighbor in the sometimes steep and arduous ways of God's service and love.

There is one such a man hidden away in a large city of this land of ours whose story may well conclude our thoughts on the Apostleship of Encouragement. He is an old man now in years and experience. Men say that in his younger days, he was the victim of a great discouragement that nearly ruined him, but by a great effort and by God's grace, he overcame the sour poison in his veins and turned it into sweetness. Now his doorstep is worn by the feet of many men and women — young men and women, for the most part — who have learned the way to that humble threshold as to a door to cheeriness and hope. And how he cheers and heartens them, that simple little old man!

The Everyday Apostle

He is stricken now by a lingering malady. He sits all day in an old armchair that his faithful man wheels around to keep it in the sunshine. But for all the twinges of pain that rack him, there is always a flute-like quality to his voice that rings like cheerful music; there is a contagious merriment in his eye that turns the blue devils out of windows and tunes up the cockles of the heart like generous wine. How much good this old man does I would not like to try to set down. How far his Apostle-ship of Encouragement has reached out into the world no one on earth can guess.

But there he sits, day in and day out, dispensing spiritual sunshine. Some of his friends suspect (but I think no one has ever dared to ask him) that a great deal of that encouraging and sympathetic temper of his is due to a resolution (an ago-nized and awful resolution it must have been) taken while he was yet sore and quivering from that great discouragement of his early years, that he would never let a chance go by to hearten and inspire the low-spirited and the timid by generous sympathy. How much happier and holier the world would soon become if everyone who has fallen victim to discourage-ment himself would straightway take a similar resolution!

For encouragement — and this reflection shall be our last — is a great deal like mercy in the poet's saying: "It blesses him who gives and him who takes." To be truly encouraging, we must keep our own soul in an atmosphere of cheery and healthy op-timism. To exorcise the imp of dejection from another, we must first shake free from his dark and ugly sway ourselves.

It is a very common counsel, when we are sad, to go and try to cheer some other mourner. Why not turn the same shrewd advice to our present matter and shake off our own discouragement, if need be, by trying to encourage someone else? What a pleasant and holy place the world would be if everyone set himself manfully to work to encourage goodness and virtue in all his neighbors! No more sorry looks and envious glances. No more chilling indifference, or carping criticism, or odious backbiting, or sneering opposition to good and virtuous deeds. But everywhere, on all hands, a sunny, cheerful goodwill and charity that warms the heart and makes virtue, goodness, and brave endeavor a hundred times easier, sturdier, and more effective. A general atmosphere, in a word, of holy and Christian charity, for, after all, true charity, truly understood, always spells encouragement.

The Apostleship
of Praise

⁊

Praise what is worthy

From the Apostleship of Encouragement, we pass on very naturally to think of the Apostleship of Praise. "Why," I think I hear someone say, "aren't they quite the same thing?" No, not quite the same, although their spheres do overlap in many places. For we may encourage a person without praising him, whereas, on the other hand, as we shall see, it is hardly possible to praise in the way we mean without at the same time giving some encouragement.

To begin with, let us hedge in our field a little. For there is praise and praise, and we must not take too wide a stint to plow out of such an expansive subject.

To praise, then, is in general to express our approval and commendation of a person or a thing. So much even the dictionary can tell us. But how many kinds and shades and subdivisions there are in praise! First, there is praise honest and sincere, and praise hollow, insincere, and of false lips merely. This last we mention only to fling it far aside, for it does no good to giver or to taker, but only evil. Then there is the hearty, whole-souled praise, which carries a conviction of our sincerity, and faint, grudging, qualified praise, such as we speak of in the good old saying about "damning with faint praise." Again, there is injudicious praise, intemperate and effusive, which spoils the truth of one saying by the exaggeration and fulsome flattery of the next; and there is timely, tactful, refined, and temperate praise, which comes easily and modestly from a sincere and unselfish heart. Last of all, and most important for our purpose, is another division — sharper and more easily recognizable, perhaps, than any of the preceding kinds — between "praising one to his face," as we say, or, in other words, between the praise we address to someone who is present and is listening to us, and praising the absent, or praising some quality or mode of action, which is a very different sort of praise indeed.

When and where it is prudent to praise a man to his face, how we should go about it, and with whom, and under what conditions, and whether it is likely to do the one we praise more good or harm — these are all questions that for the present we leave to each one's own wit and prudence to answer, for the subject does not concern us here. It is about the second sort of praise that we mean to think and argue at this present writing — to wit, the praise we give to absent persons, or to modes of action, or to virtues and achievements, and the influence which that praise has on ourselves and on our fellowmen.

It is clear that we are all concerned with the practical issues of this discussion. Are not all of us perpetually at it, praising or criticizing men, women, and things, during most of our waking hours? Scarcely a topic enters into our speech, and our personal attitude of praise or blame toward it, of commendation or disapproval, slips from us unawares. Even though we had as lief keep our personal attitude in the dark of our own minds, it will not stay hidden, but slips between our lips, or sparkles from our eyes, or peeps from the very wrinkles and publishes itself abroad whether we will or not. If, then, our praise and our dispraise have any influence on other men, we must do a great deal of good or a great deal of harm with it, as we go on about our business through our long lives in this watchful and listening world!

That our praise, our commendation and approval of other persons and of their acts and virtues, has an influence both on ourselves and on other men, who can doubt for a moment? Praise and its opposite, blame, have a tremendous moral power in forming ideals and attitudes and opinions and points of view. All of us, whether we like it or not, are moved by other men's authority and depend on their judgment and lean on their estimate of the value of things. What they praise, we are apt to esteem more highly; what they blame is lessened in our sight. If they are contemptuous or indifferent, we are very likely to be inclined to contempt or indifference, too.

As other men move us by their expressions of blame or praise, so do we, in our turn, influence and sway the thoughts of other men. We cannot express our admiration of a person or a thing without others being unconsciously inclined to value it more highly; if we depreciate or blame, we set their minds to censuring or fault-finding, too.

We may perhaps here object that we are quite too insignificant and of too slight importance for our praise or blame to have all the weight with men that has been just described. But our importance, or want of it, merely changes the reach and power of our praise. That we are obscure does not take away our influence; it merely confines it to a narrower circle. Within that circle, where we are known and loved, our praise or blame has still its own moral power, inevitable and strong.

We may convince ourselves of this very easily by taking the extreme example of a little child. Who could be more insignificant, of less authority and importance, than yonder little one of six or seven years? His elders listen to his prattled praise or blame with an amused indulgence that does not take account at all of his wee judgment in fixing the values of things. But see him among his little playfellows; his praise or blame is very weighty there! If he likes a toy or a game, if he dislikes a teacher or thinks a lesson dull and hard, he can mightily affect the public sentiment of the tiny republic of his equals, which hears his puny voice. So it is with us grown-up children, in our way. Each of us has likewise his certain circle, be it great or small, which listens with ready sympathy to his praise or blame and molds unconsciously its estimates upon his own.

Is it not clear, then, how easily we may make our praise and our blame subserve the end of helping other men? To put it simply, the principle is this: If we have influence with others, what we praise they will like and admire and desire to have some part in; and what we blame or criticize or condemn will be cheapened and lessened in their eyes.

See what a power this gives us, and what a responsibility. Our casual remarks, our praises and criticisms thrown off a hundred times a day, in chance encounters or occasional conversations, have all our lives been molding, altering, and deepening

the ideals and convictions of our fellowmen. Have we shown
our esteem of heavenly and godly ways of living? Our hearers
are the better for it. Did we base our praise or blame on mere
worldly or human standards of value? We have done our part
to lower their standards, their ideals, to our own. Hence it is,
mark you, that close friends come in time to have common
ways of judging, valuing, and esteeming those things of which
they speak to one another in praise or blame. Hence, too, the
fearful power of that bloody tyrant called Human Respect,
which is nothing else indeed than our respect for and fear of
the chorus of human praise or blame.

Perhaps this power of praise or of blame, its influence to
mold and form ideals and set desires afire, is nowhere greater
than with little ones. Children are mightily moved, beyond
what most of us dream, by what they hear their elders praising
or blaming. They have a marvelous power, almost an intu-
ition, for catching the opinions and standards of grown-ups
and for weaving them into their baby dreams and play. Preach
to them as you will of being good and honest and sincere and
pious, but if they catch from your daily praise and blame that
you really esteem other qualities far more than these, that you
esteem Mr. and Mrs. Wealthy, who are fashionable people, far
more than Mr. and Mrs. Poor, who are simple, pious folk; that
you think much more highly of Miss Evelyn Dress, who is so-
cially exclusive, than of Miss Anna Plain, who is full of charitable works and does a great deal for the poor, do you think
your abstract sermons and advice will hold out any bait to
their youthful fancies? Will they be dreaming of growing up to
be good and pious and dutiful, or will they be yearning to grow

worthy in time of such admiring words as they hear Papa and Mama give to Mrs. Wealthy and to Evelyn Dress?

Oh, how long we remember and how steadily we pursue the things we heard praised and commended when no one thought we were nearby, the praises we drank in, unsuspecting and unsuspected, with all the thirst and fervor of our childish hearts!

And now, how shall we turn this great moral power to subserve the purposes of an apostleship? First, by making our own hearts firm and true and sound as to what we should blame and what we should praise. For the world at large, this would be a desperate counsel and a disheartening beginning; how would the unbeliever know what justly to praise or blame? It is too often all one to him, truth and falsehood, good and evil. What he likes or dislikes must be the present standard of his praise or blame; indeed, vague as his convictions are, he would dare scarcely blame at all.

But the Catholic is saved this vagueness and confusion as to the standards of good and evil; his opinion and attitude on a whole range of subjects, on the deepest issues of life, are settled forever by the one fact of his wholehearted allegiance to the Church. As a loyal Catholic, he has but one attitude, and he has only to be well-instructed, consistent, and sturdy in his Catholic principles to praise well and blame well on the weightiest subjects that can arise.

Let us, then, form our praise and blame, all our candid estimates of men and things, on the solid and consistent ground of Catholic principle. Let us dare to do it; for however convinced we may be of the truth and soundness of our Catholic Faith, we shall often be sorely tempted to forsake those true and un-popular standards and to conform to the false but popular standards of the world. How sad it is — how queer it must seem, even to the non-believer, when he reflects on it — that a Catholic should judge and estimate men and things by the mere worldly values of time and of this life, when by his pro-fession of Catholicism, he should weigh them by the stan-dards of Heaven and of eternity! What a huge incongruity: to profess the doctrine of the Crucified, who came to overcome the world, and yet forever to have on our lips worldly maxims, worldly estimates, lauds of money-getting for its own sake, talk of pleasure-having for its own sake, nay, even praise of pros-perous scoundrels, of skillful evildoers who are the very foes and executioners of the Crucified!

Then, too, we must praise and blame according to our Catholic Faith and principles. And this means a distinct and long-continued struggle against our own evil leanings toward the falsely seeming good things, the standards and desires of the flesh and of the world. To praise and blame discreetly, we must go counter to our own lower inclinations. To estimate and approve all things according to the value they have in God's eyes is to go squarely against all that is ungodly in us, to conquer our own baser selves, which yearn and crave to praise the good things of this world.

Yet this only points to another good that comes of the Apostleship of Praise. For it is a blessed thing for us to put the world's standards aside and look manfully toward the eternal truths. If we could only grow accustomed to looking up at them and framing our ideas by them, how much more consistent, sensible, and Christian our thoughts and our actions would come to be! We would not then be dwelling on money and fashion, on clothes or goods or business or pleasure or barter or trade, as though these were man's last end and aim!

If we praise well, we shall come by degrees to love well, and then to act well. For what we praise, we grow to love, and we act by what we love. So if we would set ourselves manfully to praise honesty and honor, unselfish and lofty ways of living, faith, charity, gentleness, obedience, and holy deeds, and all the natural and supernatural virtues, we would come in time to love, and then to be like these things. If we praised men because they are staunch Catholics, because they bring up their children carefully in God's fear and love, because they are of sterling principle, and faithful in their way of life, we would, if we were sincere, soon come to be so, too.

There is another advantage in this practice of worthy praise: by commending noble Catholic and honorable ways of living, we in some way commit ourselves to attempt them ourselves. For every man likes to appear, and to be, consistent. If we have the courage to praise what is worthy, we gain heart to attempt to do it. If we find ourselves keeping company with high ideals, we shall begin to itch a bit to put them into action. If we have the good sense to speak consistently with our Catholic faith and principle, we shall grow more ashamed of going counter to them in our deeds.

There are one or two practical applications of the truths we have been dwelling on. One has to do with the way Catholics speak of other Catholics, or of Catholic enterprises and societies, or of Catholic ecclesiastics and the rulers of the Church. It is a sad thing to say, but a spirit is abroad nowadays to speak rather disparagingly of things Catholic, merely from a desire, it may be, of standing well with the world, or of showing our own broadmindedness; or perhaps, of giving other folks an idea that we are rather above the common run of the faithful, and not to be classed with the poor, ordinary Catholics we see in such numbers in church!

Leaving aside the many reasons drawn from loyalty and reverence and charity and consistency and good feeling, which rise up to condemn this unworthy attitude of mind, how unwise and injurious it is when we look at it from the viewpoint of its effect on the non-Catholics around us! They expect that we, who pledge our whole faith and stake all our hopes of life eternal on the truth, the nobleness, and the heavenly beauty of Catholic teaching, should be filled with reverence and esteem for all that belongs to or is associated with our holy Faith. They realize that we are the natural defenders and advocates of all things Catholic. How shocked and disillusioned and repelled they must be to find us speaking in a depreciating way of our brothers in the cause of Christ, of our pastors, who bear His authority, of the persons and things that are most intimately associated with His Church, His spiritual kingdom in this world!

How sternly we should crush in ourselves this mean and carping spirit; how steadily we should urge ourselves to lean toward praise and encouragement whenever there is question of Catholics or of Catholic enterprise! No need of false praise or of fulsome adulation, for these things are never helpful or good. If we have clear eyes and an unenvious heart, we shall always find enough and to spare in the Catholic world around us to furnish us with many an occasion for hearty and merited commendation.

Again, a failing of ours that must often hurt and scandalize the well-disposed non-Catholic is that queer tendency we have to set up as representative Catholics men who are poor types indeed of what the Church desires in her sons. Because a man owns to the name of Catholic and has won place and esteem in the world, by his profession, it may be, or his fortune or his wits, we are often all too ready to trumpet him abroad as a great Catholic citizen and point to him with pride as a bright example of his kind.

What must the non-believer think, once more, when he knows quite well that this man's whole claim to distinction and esteem rests on his possession of the good things of this world; that he is good and great, if so at all, only from a worldly standpoint, and that if he is viewed from a sound Catholic viewpoint and weighed in the balance of Catholic principle, he is one of the least worthy and estimable of the Church's sons?

"And this is the manner of man," the non-Catholic will say to himself, "whom these Catholics set up as their representative, their boast, and their pride! God save the mark! They are the most inconsistent people on earth. They praise unworldliness and honor this shameless worldling; they speak of piety and extol this notorious neglecter of his religious duties; they prate of honesty and sober living, and then join hands with this successful rogue! I will have none of them. They cannot believe the noble things they say!"

Let us be careful — very circumspect and careful — about whom or what we set aloft as representative of our Catholic principles! We are watched, and we are judged by a keen-sighted, shrewdly suspicious, and not overly friendly world!

We have reached the limits we had set ourselves and have scarcely yet broken the surface of this vast subject of the power of praise. But what we have said will have fulfilled its purpose if it serves only to make us realize how great and far-reaching is the influence that our blame or our commendation wields on the minds of other men.

We walk through the world, quite carelessly it may be, speaking out our minds, proclaiming our opinions, giving forth our standards, little conscious all the while of how much our light words may mean in the ears of our fellows. Those words we utter — the praise, the criticism, the censure, and the blame — go abroad into other minds and hearts and are caught up and repeated and multiplied like ripples in still water, until the thoughts of a whole multitude of men and women and children are wrought upon, their standards raised or lowered, their emulation and their desire stirred up and fired for weal or woe. Who but God can tell how far each easy, careless speech of ours has been borne abroad and swayed men's minds and fortunes? Such a mighty power for good or for evil lies hidden in the tiny organ we call our tongue!

Apostleship of
Speech in Business

☞

Conduct yourself in a holy way
in your workplace

We sometimes say that professional men are liable to grow abstracted and overly engrossed in their own special line. If we observe a bit more closely, I think we shall find that it is the man of business who becomes most deeply wrapped up in the affairs of his traffic and his gain. Listen to the talk on the some fine morning when men's tongues are loosened by the weather or the time of year and see for yourself what makes the chief matter of their casual talk.

The professional man will speak of many things quite foreign to his specialty — of current happenings in this or other lands, of the last book, or the latest rumor of war. But the businessman, in nine cases out of ten, is rattling on either about politics, which is a sort of secondary business with him, or about his beloved trade. What he has bought or sold or is just about to buy or sell, the profits he has made or is expecting, the chances of markets, the changes in supply and demand — you may hear all these things discussed to no end with the greatest gusto, with never a word of any alien topic whatsoever thrown in on either side to relieve the monotony of the talk of shop.

The Everyday Apostle

This perpetual abstraction and absorption in matters of dollars and cents is, to put it mildly, no very ennobling thing for the mind and heart. A man must live, to be sure, and he must have money to live; but to be forever busy with thoughts of money is not very much more elevating than to be always busy with thoughts of food.

Even from the low standpoint of our own mental saneness and efficiency, then, it would be very useful to make some practical reflections on the subject of the Apostleship of Speech in Business.

But there are other motives for dwelling on the subject, which are weightier than this. To begin with, it is sometimes rather pointedly questioned nowadays whether our Catholic businessmen are the mighty instruments for spreading their holy Faith that we might expect them to be from their numbers and their general influence. When our Lord said that His followers should be the salt of the earth and the light of the world, He did not mean, of course, that we were all to preach His gospel from the housetops, but it is quite certain that He did mean that everyone was to do his share in spreading the good tidings among men.

Suppose that a Catholic spends ten, twenty, or fifty years of his life in the closest kind of daily and hourly contact with all sorts and conditions of men, and that at the end of that long time of constant opportunity, he cannot point to any deliberate or consistent work for the spreading abroad of the truth of Christ. Can that man by any stretching of the meaning of words be properly said to have discharged his Christian duty of being the salt of the earth and the light of the world?

Conduct yourself in a holy way in your workplace

At this point in our reflections, I seem to hear some hard-headed man of business break in upon me with an emphatic objection: "Anyone who would speak of business life as a time of constant opportunity for spreading Catholic truth cannot be very familiar with what he is talking about. Why, a business-man would laugh at you if you were to begin that sort of thing. An office or a store is the last place on earth to do any mission-ary work in the way of spreading Catholic doctrine. The Apos-tleship of Speech is all very well at home, in social life, or even in professional life, if you will, but it is out of place altogether in the busy and distracted day of the average businessman."

Let us go over the ground a bit together, my dear objector, and see whether all opportunities are wanting even in the busy haunts of trade. First, there is the negative side of the picture to be looked at, for we accomplish nearly as much good at times by the things we refrain from as by the things we do. Whether he likes it or not, the man who professes to be a Catholic is al-ways under scrutiny. Men differ in many things, but for the most part they agree in this, that they despise a hypocrite and resent a man's making profession of a high and holy creed, and then acting and speaking no better than the common run. And so they keep a sharper watch on Catholics (who, as they know perfectly well, profess the hardest and loftiest religion in the world) to see whether they make at least some decent ef-fort to live up to their exalted principles. This thought opens up to us at once a rich and varied field for reflection, which, of course, we shall have time to travel over only very briefly.

It goes without saying, to begin with, that a Catholic man's speech should be utterly pure from any taint of that monstrous abuse of man's faculty of speech that we call profanity. To hear even a pagan making free with the holiest words in our language, to lend a little emphasis to his worthless remarks, is dreadful enough, even though we may offer for him the sorry excuse that he does not realize the evil thing he is doing. But to hear a Catholic employing in light and ribald jest the sacred names he learned to reverence at his mother's knee is sad and shameful in the extreme.

There are, however, more subtle and insidious ways than this of giving scandal in our talk, which the Apostleship of Speech will make an earnest Catholic avoid. One of these — by no means the least dangerous and harmful — is the way we are liable to fall into making free with another man's good name.

In this age of unlicensed speech, many folk seem almost to have lost the sense of right and wrong in dealing with their neighbor's reputation. They speak quite freely of his faults and failings; they even publish his hidden sins. Nothing is easier to acquire than this fatal habit of making free with other people's good name, but how little most men realize the sinister consequences of their fluent slander! How little they think of the reparation they are bound to make for the good repute they have unjustly stolen and for the scandal they have given by their loose and libelous speech.

The average pagan may again offer in excuse of this evil habit of calumny and slander the slim defense that the evil of his ways has not been pointed out to him with all the clearness and force of Christ's divine teaching, but only in the vaguer warnings of the natural law. But how can we Catholics justify ourselves — we, who have heard from the incarnate God Himself such words as these: "Thou shalt not bear false witness"; "Judge not lest ye be judged"; "If ye did it to the least of these, my brethren, you did it unto me"?[9]

Yet in the off-hand familiarity of the office or the store, we may find many an occasion to fall into this abominable habit of uncharitable talk. We are abstracted, worried, or tired, and our mind and our tongue both crave a bit of ready, interesting speech. Nothing easier in the world than to talk of persons whom we know! Nothing nearer, alas, to our poor lips than a morsel of acrimonious criticism, or an unsavory rumor about one of our acquaintances! So we say the word or two to our neighbor, and he or she takes up the strain, and perhaps even the topic becomes general, as each one adds a bit of fretful or unkind comment of his own. Then we go back to work, feeling refreshed, it may be, at having gotten rid of so much rancor; but we little realize the evil we have done.

The chances are that in those few moments, we have done our neighbor a serious, maybe an irreparable, wrong. We have planted the fruitful seeds of aversion and suspicion in our hearers' hearts. The memory of our words and even of the occasion that called them forth may die away from their minds. The very manner of our disparaging and calumnious speech may vanish from their thoughts. But when hereafter the name of the person we spoke ill of comes to their ears, the lingering prejudice born of our unkind talk will rise up, and they will dislike and distrust him.

[9] Cf. Exod. 20:16; Matt. 7:1, 25:40.

The Everyday Apostle

Now, what is the keen, observant man of business likely to think of men who profess a creed of the tenderest charity and goodwill toward all of God's children and yet soil their lips with these vile calumnies?

Another sort of talk that the Catholic man or woman in business should be solicitous to avoid is what we might call for short a sort of lip-worship of mammon. To hear some businessmen of the day, you would think that the sole person to be admired is the successful money-getter and that the last end of mankind is to gather worldly gear. They speak of wealthy men with bated breath; they praise the wiles of the unscrupulous financier with an approving and an envying air. You gather from their ordinary talk that in their eyes the happy man is he who can keep his stealings well beyond the purview of the law. Even these worshipers of sharp dealing will hardly be much edified, I think, to find the Catholic men and women of their acquaintance joining in their loose views of the seventh commandment. They know well enough that, in our system of belief, goods and gold are only means toward the heavenly and everlasting kingdom, and not ends to be pursued at the cost of body and soul. They know, too, quite well that a Catholic is bound to repent and to give back his ill-gotten gains before he can validly receive the sacrament of Penance. What must they think, then, when they hear us speak the same loose and worldly language with as they do?

Another fault that we should dwell on a bit (although our catalog is rather long already) is the way — alas, too common — in which some Catholics speak of persons and of things pertaining to their Church and their Faith. Here, again,

Conduct yourself in a holy way in your workplace

we must try to realize the marked difference between us and the followers of all other creeds. In other creeds, it has come at last to this: that men look upon their ministers as pretty much on the same plane as themselves, appointed by merely human authority and governing and teaching only with the influence that each one's talents and good qualities can claim.

Everyone knows quite well that here, as in so many other points, the Catholic belief is altogether different. We profess that, however humble the talents of our priests may be, and whatever their personal character, we are bound to see in each of them the ambassador and vicegerent of God, who has put them where they are. Any insult we offer to them in their priestly office is offered to the very dignity and holiness with which they have been endowed by God. How strangely inconsistent, then, it must seem to those outside the fold to hear us discussing and criticizing our pastors!

Even if we were to do or say nothing positive and definite on the subject of our Catholic Faith, but were to content ourselves with avoiding the evils and abuses we have been pointing out, we would have accomplished a great deal in the way of a true apostleship. For the world at large, used as it is to hear all manner of slander and criticism and the common malice and uncharitableness that make up so much of the speech of men, will be struck with wonder at the spectacle of a man or woman whose talk is quite innocent of all offense, and will be moved by that rare and singular effect to esteem and inquire into our Faith, which is the motive of so much self-restraint and careful reverence for the laws of God. Thus, even though we seem to have little time or opportunity for anything like an apostleship during the full days of business, here is at least one way in which we may all become apostles: by never doing or saying anything unworthy of our Catholic principles, by making an effort to attend at least to the negative side of the Apostleship of Speech in Business.

The Apostleship
of Character

⌒

Wear a Catholic face

In the last chapter, we dwelled in some detail on what we called the negative side of the Apostleship of Speech in Business: the ways in which we may aid the Church's cause among men by keeping ourselves clear of certain prevalent and common sins and abuses of speech. There remains great matter for useful observation on the positive side of that selfsame subject, to which we shall now address ourselves.

In the previous chapter, we asked whether such an apostleship has any place in the hurry and flurry of business life. As the speediest and most effective way of answering this pertinent inquiry, let us plunge at once into a discussion of some of the practical ways in which ordinary Catholic men or women, in shop or office or factory, may help by their daily speech to spread the kingdom of God on earth.

Our first suggestion shall be a practical and momentous one of wide and various application, and with a bearing not only on this present matter of daily speech (which is, after all, only one, although perhaps the chief one, of our ways of manifesting our thoughts and character), but on all our dealings with our fellowmen. And the suggestion is this: Let us begin by always putting on a Catholic face before the world! A short sentence and easily written — but in need of how much qualifying and explanation!

What do we mean by putting on a Catholic face before the world? We do not mean that we should be arrogant, or intolerant, or pugnacious about being Catholics; not that we should throw it into our neighbor's teeth, or drag our Catholicism forth at unseasonable times, to be a rag of controversy or a provocation to our non-Catholic fellows; or even that we should talk of our Catholicism as an attribute or quality of ourselves, as though it were a great credit to us that we are Catholics, with the mild and obvious implication to all dissenters that it is a great shame and pity to them that they are not. All these ways of acting, and many others that savor of the same arrogance, selfishness, and personal vanity, may, by some stretching of language, be called putting on a "Catholic" face — but not such a Catholic face as our saying recommends. We mean a very different sort of face indeed. For all these ways of acting only advertise the selfish and partial viewpoint that Catholicism belongs to us.

The attitude we mean to recommend is quite the converse one: that all of us — heart, mind, body, and soul — belong to Catholicism! The spirit that we should have is quiet, modest, tactful, and unintruding. It is as gentle as it is fearless, as kind and persuasive as it is uncompromising, where there is question of principle or truth. The man or woman who puts on this sort of a Catholic face goes through the world professing his Faith in every daily action, because he or she is known by every acquaintance to be a sturdy, prudent, and staunch believer in and defender of the holy Catholic Church.

To convey this impression, and to let everyone know quite plainly that we are, first and foremost, Catholics in heart and soul, no great parade or forced endeavor is required. What is necessary is a deep, true, and unreserved interior loyalty to the Church and to her doctrines and her rulers, and a firm, modest and consistent way of acting along the lines of our principles and our beliefs. There is something in the wholesome moral atmosphere that a true-hearted Catholic bears about him, which has a solemn eloquence to proclaim his Faith to his fellowmen. And the businessman, or clerk, or shop-girl, or factory-hand, or the servant in a private home who keeps this attitude of quiet, earnest, and determined Catholic spirit and principle will need to make use of few formal proclamations to announce to everyone with whom he or she has any dealings that here is a practical and sincere Catholic, prepared and determined to do whatever that great and holy name implies and requires.

If we carry into our daily life of business such a Catholic face, such a Catholic attitude and bearing of body and soul as we have outlined here, our work of the Apostleship of Speech will be half accomplished already. For, as we have noted before, we speak by actions, by bearing, character, and manners, much more loudly and eloquently sometimes than by any mere noise of words. And without the speech of action, the speech of words is mostly vain and ineffective; for as compared with the latter, as all men realize, the former kind of speech is incomparably more certain, earnest, and sincere.

The Everyday Apostle

There are some further consequences of "wearing a Catholic face" in our business life that have an even more direct bearing on our present subject and hence invite us to a more detailed consideration. To wear such a character before the world tends to make earnest men come to us of their own accord, to inquire about our holy Faith. We do not realize, I am afraid, those of us who are busied all day long with the clatter and clink of dollars and cents on the dusty counters of trade, how weary, lonely, and starving the souls of many even of our prosperous and well-fed fellows are for the bread that Christ came to break to the children of men, for the living water that He alone could offer to the parched lips of an eager and thirsty world.

In the midst of their material success, their lust for gain, and their eagerness for the ventures and excitements of business life, most men have vacant moments and weary stretches of emptiness and longing. Something within their bosoms tells them that they were, after all, not made only for the present and perishable world. Something higher and nobler in them stirs restlessly and craves for the Infinite and the Eternal, and they look about with longing and uneasy eyes for some guide, some hint, some token, some finger-post to set them on the path toward God and Heaven. They yearn for some clue out of their labyrinth of temporal affairs into the pure air of God's spiritual dominion, into the kingdom of the spirit, which somehow, somewhere, He must have set up in this world. It is in those better moments that there shines forth the brightest opportunity to save and purify and strengthen these fellowmen and women of yours by pointing out to them the way into that Church which has the clue to all their questions, the balm for all their restless ills and cares.

If their wandering eyes do not see any guide out of their empty longings, any deliverer to point out the way to better things, their happy hour will pass. The dust and fog of earthly concerns will close once more around their spirit, the Heaven-sent longing will fade away, and all their energies will sink down and become engrossed once more in the sordid interests of this present life. But if they have seen in you this sterling Catholic spirit of which we speak, then in their moments of spiritual longing, your face will rise up before them as the face of one who has some holy clue to the weary riddles of life; they will come to you — timidly, cautiously, it may be, even the boldest of them throwing out delicate hints, giving you subtle invitations to aid them in their search after light. Sometimes it will be only some seemingly careless question they will have to ask you; sometimes they will make a passionate appeal for you to tell them of the truth.

Then, if you are a true Catholic, a true and sterling man or woman, this is your golden opportunity. Then you may use, indeed, to do a golden deed, the holy powers of the Apostleship of Speech. Quietly, prudently, tactfully, speaking humbly and earnestly with the eloquence of a grateful and believing heart, you may bear witness, as the Apostles did of old, to the Faith that is in you. You may put this searching soul on the true path of salvation and set his mind and heart on the way to find the fullness of Catholic truth.

Does all this sound utopian and visionary, too strange and too delightful ever to be true? But it has happened, time and time again, thank God, here in our own country, even among our poorest toilers in the great mill or the busy factory.

"Tell me your secret, Mary," cried a haggard-looking girl to the Catholic shoe-worker who stood beside her. "How do you keep so good among us, some of whom are so dreadfully bad? I'm sick of all this wicked talk myself. Tell me your secret; how you manage to keep clean of it?" And do you think Mary had any trouble then in pouring forth to that ready listener her simple story of the strength, consolation, and support she found in her Catholic Faith?

As to the matter of our Catholic speech to our friends, it must arise, like eloquence in Daniel Webster's definition, from the man, the hearer, and the occasion. Our tact and sympathy should tell us how far to go, what to say, and what to leave unsaid. Surely we do not need any hard and fast rules or guideposts to direct us in speaking to our own friends of the subject that should be nearest and dearest to our hearts.

Yet, excellent as this sounds in theory, in practice the matter is by no means so smooth and easy. Two things will help us immensely: knowledge and kindness. To be effective apostles, as we have said before, we must know thoroughly the elements of Catholic belief and the Catholic attitude on questions of moment of the day. To do this, we must read Catholic books on Catholic subjects and Catholic views. We must take an interest in Catholic periodicals. We must, in a word, steep our thoughts in a Catholic atmosphere. Then Catholic truth will flow easily and naturally from our lips.

Second, there is that other requisite: heartfelt and sympathetic kindness. The great heart of the world is really sad and lonely. The hilariousness, distraction, and pretense of our modern men are really only a frantic effort to escape from a great inner hunger and loneliness. To reach that aching heart and minister the balm of truth and consolation, we must have recourse to gentleness, sympathy, and kindness. The heart of man, to use a fine old figure, is like a delicate flower: it will not open to burly blasts and tempests of disputation; but let the genial sun and the soft winds of friendliness and kindness shine and blow, and it opens wide to drink the warmth and light, and gives forth grateful fragrance.

If we but fulfill these three conditions in our own person; if we wear a Catholic face before the world, and supply our minds with the riches of Catholic thought and principle, and fill ourselves — our whole selves — with true charity, tenderness, and kindness, the Apostleship of Speech will grow easy for us indeed.

"Hard conditions!" you say. So are all conditions hard that lead to noble enterprises. It was never easy to win souls to God. Christ, our Lord, did not find it easy to walk, footsore and weary, through the harsh ways of Israel, repeating an unwelcome message in the ears of an unwilling world. Peter and Paul, and all the holy Twelve, did not find it an easy task to range over rude lands and across dangerous seas to save the nations given over to all lewdness, frivolity, and crime. The countless army of God's ministers does not find it easy to lead laborious lives in the midst of weariness and privation to bring men's rebellious necks under the meek yoke of Christ.

Do you, my dear Catholic man or woman, cry out in surprise that you are not worthy to be spoken of along with these?

The Everyday Apostle

You must endure it. To you, even if you are the lowliest, simplest, most ignorant among us, were spoken also those stirring yet warning words from His own lips: "You are the salt of the earth; you are the light of the world; you are a city seated on a mountain; let your light shine before men";[10] and most solemn, momentous, and significant of all, those words which all of us, great and small, teachers and taught, shall hear from the lips of the Great Judge on the day of the Last Judgment: "Amen, I say unto you, as long as you did it unto one of these, my least brethren, you did it unto me."[11]

[10] Cf. Matt. 5:13, 14, 16.
[11] Matt. 25:40.

The Apostleship
of Counsel

☙

Steer others
away from error

Somewhere in our romantic colonial history is told a very pitiful story. One of those crews of hardy adventurers who crossed
the dangerous ocean to tap the riches of the new continent
came upon a river whose very sands were gold. There it lay —
the precious, beautiful stuff, piled up in glistening heaps, all
ready for their eager fingers, and they fell to work with glee.
They gathered sackfuls and barrelfuls, laughing at the hard-
ships and the toil, until their vessels were loaded down with
the treasure. Then they sailed happily homeward over the perilous sea. And when, after many a storm and many an hour of
wretched and anxious toil, they got safely into port, full of
comfort and cheer, they spread the wonderful news abroad
that they had brought unheard-of riches back with them.

So men from the shore, skilled in metal, came eagerly out
to look at the golden hoard. They peered into the sacks of
treasure, plunged in their trembling hands, and let the dust
run down in golden streams against the sunlight. Then they
turned to the exultant homecomers with scorn and anger in
their eyes.

"This is the wealth of the New World?" they cried. "Did you ask us out to look at this? It is all only a base ore of iron, you unspeakable simpletons! All your hard-got treasure is nothing but fool's gold!"

And it was so. The weary, dangerous voyaging, the searching and toil, the tedious passage home had all been only for this. They had a cargo of worthless pyrites; all their labor had gotten them only so much paltry fool's gold.

A pitiful story, surely. We feel a pang of sympathy only to think of it. All that expectancy and labor, and the bitter awakening at the end! Yet within the circle of our own experience, under our very eyes, we often see an even sadder and more tragic folly. For there are many earnest and laborious men and women nowadays, as in all days, who in their own deluded way are sedulous gatherers of shining rubbish; adventurous voyagers and patient toilers, it may be, but bringers home of nothing but fool's gold.

There is the unhappy man who will tell you that he is quite satisfied with doing his duty by his neighbor, and banning no man, and living as a decent fellow should. He does not see any special need of a definite religion. He never cared much, anyway, for ceremonies and observances and doctrine. A good, clean, upright life is quite enough for him.

And so he does, sometimes, go to great lengths and make costly efforts and sacrifices to lead a clean and honorable life as the world sees it. Perhaps he is by nature kindly and courteous, generous and just; and his days go by in fair and noble appearance, and he makes a show of good and worthy deeds. But, alas, for all the outward glitter and show of goodness! He is only gathering heaps of silly treasure, painfully loading the precious vessel of his soul with the worthless freight of base fool's gold. There is no substance in his pretentious virtue if it lacks the precious touch of the love and service of God. There is no merit in his godless goodness, because it is done for man and man's eye only; it has not the weight and luster of the golden grace of God.

Again, there is the man who has been brought up in an alien creed, yet comes one day to see that in the Catholic Church, and there alone, is the fullness of God's truth. But he demurs when conscience tells him, "Your place is there!" "Oh," he answers, "not yet! There will be time enough later. There will be ample opportunity for such a change when I am older and more interested in religious thought. God cannot mean me to turn the whole current of my life awry just at this time — this especially inconvenient time. Let me bide awhile where I am. Why should I put myself in such a pother the very moment I find out something new? And, in the meantime, can I not go on leading a good, devout, even a fervent, life here in the church in which I was born? There is a good deal of truth to be found in my religion, too. I could serve God better as a Catholic? Very true, but can I not serve Him quite well here?"

Fool's gold! When a person lingers on in bad faith where he knows that God does not wish him to be, his specious show of fervor and zeal are worth nothing. He may indeed put on all the outward shine and glitter of a Christian life. He may multiply observance on observance and offer many works that God does not require, to balance out his slowness in the one thing God demands. But in the eyes of Heaven, are not his acts only a mockery of justice and goodness? Hard words! Yet are they not sadly and pitifully true? Cannot God see in these pious works the tinsel glitter of insincerity? Is not such a man willfully delving in the deceitful river-sands of heresy and error, instead of the deep mines of truth, and bringing up, with all his sweat and labor, only fool's gold to meet the eyes of God?

Again (and this is the saddest case of all), there is the fallen-away Catholic, who was once faithful, earnest, and devout, but has let his fervor and service dwindle slowly into tepidity and carelessness. He lives quite frankly a godless life, just as does the pagan world around him. He does not deny the Faith in theory, but he calmly disregards it in practice. Its restraints and observances are far too rigid, too uneasy and exacting for his idea of comfort and of peace. And yet in his secret heart, he cherishes a hope that he may somehow serve both God and mammon, that God will somehow be content with the good he does, and not be too strict and stern with him for the good he fails to do. He has a lingering expectation that his honest life, his kindness to his friends, his doing harm to no man, may raise him just as safely to Heaven as some of those anxious folk who never miss Mass on Sunday and are so solicitous in keeping the precepts of the Church. Is not his fair-dealing a glorious and goodly thing? Are not his courtesy and good feeling holy and blessed, and will not his clean life here be found worthy of the eternal life to come?

Fool's gold! What is all this material goodness in the eyes of God, who has deigned to make known the very precise and definite service that He jealously requires, and who finds that wished-for service insolently slighted and denied? What would an employer think or say if he found his employee taking his own ease and pleasure, doing his own sweet will in everything, and seeking to make up for this neglect of duty by pleasant manners and a winning smile? Surely, he who has known the fullness of supernatural truth, and who turns from the practice of our blessed Faith to seek his happiness here and hereafter in the empty exercise of merely natural and pagan virtues, is of all men the vainest gatherer of vainest dross against the dreadful day of God!

And so we might go on with example after example of men nowadays who carry on the outward show of a blameless and upright life, but those works are mockery and their good deeds a delusion for want of the touch of grace and faith, for lack of the true ring and luster of heavenly merit that only grace and faith can give.

But what have all these reflections to do with us others, who are neither condemners of religion nor followers of an alien creed? Only this: we know, or we should know, very clearly the false gold from the true.

Suppose there had been with those hapless adventurers some man skilled in metallurgy, who could have told at a glance the false gold from the real. Would it not have been a crying shame, a terrible sin in him, not to call out, and protest, and warn the deluded crew that they were wasting their trouble and their toil? Would it not have been simple madness for him to have acquiesced in their vain delight, and caught the prevalent enthusiasm, and sympathized with their fool's joy in their fool's treasure?

Yet how many Catholic men and women who know full well that those who are near and dear to them are living in a fool's paradise of delusion and heaping up worthless and tinsel deeds against the great trying day, are deaf to the kindness and duty that bids them warn these gatherers of fool's gold?

"Oh, he is so good, so upright, so generous," we hear them say of these deluded ones. "Why, he is better than many Catholics; why should I trouble him with advice?" Why tell him, in other words, that he is heaping up false treasures, bogus gold? Why say the word of warning and remonstrance? Why show our uneasiness, our distress and disapproval of this squandering of precious lives, this wasting of effort and time that will never count for Heaven?

We do not act so, as we have said before, in matters where earthly treasure is in question, where money, lands, and goods are at stake. If we see a friend of ours wasting his toil in a bogus venture, or spending good money on worthless stock, we hurry and give him the word. May we not do as much in matters of eternal moment, when the gold at stake is the gold of heavenly merit, with which a man must buy of his God the kingdom without end?

Is not this one reason so many Catholics fall away little by little from all pious observance and go down by gentle grades, down the easy slope of indifference to the sloughs of unbelief, because their own people, who live at their side, do not reach out a hand in time to save them?

They remark, of course, the first beginnings: the youthful piety growing cold, the old fidelity at Mass and at Communion waxing slack and poor. Now a Sunday morning abed, no holy

Mass; now a slighting word about sacred things that shows that the soul is growing cold. If we would only aid them then! If we would only stop them there in the first steps of their downward course, when a little leap would put them on the sunny heights again.

We need not take them aside and put on a solemn look and lecture them. Often that would be a most silly and ineffective way. But a quiet word, when we see their ears are open and their heart is ready, a sorrowful look when we feel sure they will understand. Not many words are necessary when a friend speaks lovingly to his friend.

And if we, their own friends, their own people, refuse this easy, necessary work of love, who else under Heaven is to attend to it? God has put them in our hands, as He puts all men into the hands of other men. Can a stranger do it? Can even the priest? How is he to know of the small and faint beginnings? When he is besought to work a change, the harm is already done. Our friend, whom we could have saved when his evil course was just commencing, has now strayed far away from Church and priest and altar; he hears all pious exhortations with a hard air of self-sufficient unbelief.

Little by little, the fervor of his youth cooled away; but now he is quite cold. The priest, who could not have hindered the evil, can scarcely begin to cure it now. Only you, whose word, whose look, might have kept off the mortal sickness, only you can bring it medicine. You must begin, even now, now at this late and evil day, and little by little win him back again.

"But we must be prudent and tactful and discreet! It does not do to speak much on such subjects; we may so easily do more harm than good! Rather than say or do too much, isn't it often better to let such folks alone?"

Yes, by all means, let us be prudent and discreet, but when were such precious gifts as prudence and tact required for such an easy thing as merely letting our erring friends alone? Indifference and laziness would seem quite sufficient for that. No, our tact and prudence may come into glorious play in choosing the time and the manner of bringing them to see the sad emptiness of their fictitious virtue, the sad delusion of their sedulous gatherings of base fool's gold! There we may find grand scope for every particle of prudence and tact that we have got or God has given us!

In sober truth, it is a difficult task to open men's eyes to their own amazing folly and point out to them the worthlessness of their laborious lives, spent apart from the will and the service of God. It is a task we might well refuse to enter on at all, were not men's very souls the stake for which we toil. But God has put our brothers' destiny into the hands of us other men and set us near them to warn them — tactfully, discreetly always — lest they waste all their precious lives in gathering fool's gold!

Let us not suffer our own sloth or reluctance or false diffidence to hold us back, where we see our duty clear and recognize the urgent need. For we may quiet our consciences now, and justify our own non-interference with many specious arguments; but what will our friends whom we have not warned and counseled say to us, think of us, when they have got past that moment of terrible awakening and revelation which is the lightning-flash of the judgment of God?

"You knew and you did not tell us, you saw and you did not cry out in warning and fear! You let us, your own people, fill our hands with false and bogus riches, gather up for the eye of a Judge who knows no deceiving the worthless dross and ore that has no price or value in Heaven! All the while you knew that we should go poor and naked and mean before the eye of God. And yet you left us so long to gather the tinsel of seeming good works without love or grace or merit. Fool's gold! Oh, you unkind friend!"

The Apostleship
of Charity

Assist those in need

Is it not enough to make us tremble to see how many otherwise good, and even fervent, Catholics habitually neglect Christ's solemn admonition to help the poor? "The poor indeed you have always with you,"[12] so we seldom can plead a lack of opportunity for putting into practice the grave commandment of our Lord.

In town and country, now as ever, they are always with us, needy and numerous — not only the poor who have become so by their own fault or negligence, but the innocent poor, the victims of a mother's sloth or a father's crime. What excruciating miseries they suffer! The weakness of hunger, the agonies of shame, the pang of anxious uncertainty as to whence shall come their evening's shelter and tomorrow's food; the hopelessness of utter indigence: these are often with them and threaten them always.

The child wails to his mother for food, but the mother herself is faint with hunger. The mother sees her little ones

[12] John 12:8.

perishing from want and shivering with cold, and she weeps before her husband and their father.

But he, too, perhaps, is crushed with poverty and feeble with disease, and he looks on in despairing agony, unable to relieve them. They cry aloud to their Father in Heaven, who has compassion on the least thing that lives and who hears the young ravens when they call to Him for food. But that infinitely merciful and tender Father is a God of order and of law, and He has given man into man's keeping and put the relief of the wretched into the hands of his fellowmen.

It is to us, then, that the hungry and destitute must turn at last, as to their appointed saviors from misery and distress. Do we minister to them in tenderness and compassion, or are we so thoughtless in our comfortable plenty, as to deny these wretched ones the little aid they seek? Ah, when our own children gather around us, clean and fair and merry, well-clad and well-housed against cold and storm, innocent of hunger and of shame, we must let our thoughts wander in pity from their bright looks, safe as they are in the sheltered ways of happy childhood, to the wretched shanty where lurk the squalid children of the poor. Christ prays us to have pity, at least upon the little ones; to take compassion in a practical way, on neglected children, ragged, shivering and weeping, cold and hungry, ignorant, it may be, and abandoned. The leavings of many a table would make them a banquet; the cast-off clothing of richer little ones would be a decent covering to wrap their wasted limbs; a little part of the money spent in mere indulgence would mean to them very life, and happiness, and cheerful hope.

But this is not all. There is another thought that, to some of us, may prove more piercing and more moving still. We are the almoners of God. He has given man into the hands of man, and made each one's brother his keeper. "Love thy neighbor" is second only to "Love thy God."

Now, the wail of the starving poor is going up forever around us, and near us, even at our very doors. What meaning has that incessant, piteous crying of hungry hearts and of hungry bodies, in the ever-listening ears of God? Alas! May it not be an unceasing although unconscious accusation — an indictment uttered loud and strong against us at the dreadful bar of the Most High? And shall we answer to that charge, that we were thoughtless and distracted and busied with our own concerns, when we have such commands and often-repeated warnings? Or is this a light duty, to be easily disregarded, or a trifling opportunity for merit, to be readily forgotten, when Christ Himself has declared, "Amen, I say unto you, as long as you did it to one of these, my least brethren, you did it unto me. As long as you did it not to one of these, my least brethren, you did it not unto me"?[13]

Would that it were only the very rich in this world's goods who stood in danger of this grave charge and stern accounting! Would that those of us were at least exempt who are poor ourselves and can scarcely give an alms in money or in food! But the precept is most broad: the needy are without number, their wants, various and manifold, so that there is not one of us who cannot give alms of some sort, if willing to do so, and

[13] Matt. 25:40, 45.

there is not one of us who can give who is not held by this command of God. Nor does our personal inability to minister to the poor excuse us, for there is the Society of St. Vincent de Paul, and many other charitable societies, ready to be our vicar; nor does even the lack of earthly goods acquit us, for we can give at least the alms of prayer.

God speaks, it is true, as we speak most commonly, of corporal aid and comfort, but these, after all, are things of lesser import — types and figures of the aid we owe to our neighbor's spirit; of the alms we should give, of love to his needy heart, of faith to his starving soul. God speaks in terms of temporal aid for this further reason also: that the body must be fed and clothed before the spirit can be strengthened, and he who lets his neighbor thirst, or starve, or lie uncared for in sickness or imprisonment, when he might easily aid him, will scarcely have the countenance to pretend concern for his sick heart or lonely soul.

It is, then, salutary for us all to read this precept over, as it is written in many ways and for many ages, by prophets, sages, and saints, and to take it practically to heart. And there is perhaps no other place in the whole cycle of the Scriptures where its weight is forced upon us so emphatically as in the description of that last great Judgment, where the warnings of the Eternal reach a sanction and a summing up in the momentous sentence to be pronounced on man, before he goes forth to everlasting joy or woe. How strange in our ears are the warning words of that sentence, as Christ has told them to us. "Then shall the King say to them that shall be on His right hand: 'Come, ye blessed of my Father, possess you the kingdom prepared for you from the foundation of the world. For I was hungry, and you gave me to eat; I was thirsty, and you gave me to drink; I was a stranger, and you took me in: naked, and you covered me: sick, and you visited me: I was in prison, and you came to me.' Then He shall say to them also that shall be on His left hand: 'Depart from me, you cursed . . . for I was hungry and you gave me not to eat . . . naked, and you covered me not, sick and in prison and you did not visit me.' Then they also shall answer Him, saying: 'Lord, when did we see Thee hungry, or thirsty, or a stranger, or naked, or sick, or in prison, and did not minister to Thee?' Then He shall answer them, saying: 'Amen, I say to you, as long as you did it not to one of these least, neither did you do it to me.' And these shall go into everlasting punishment: but the just, into life everlasting."[14]

No word here of murder, or blasphemy, or the seven deadly sins; or any of those offenses from which in our inward searchings we are likely to thank Heaven we are so free. No, but the just are to be rewarded and the wicked to be condemned on this strange standard: "Have you fed the hungry, clothed the naked, visited the sick and the imprisoned? Have you pitied the wretched and needy with an active pity, and succored them in their distress?"

Not that other good deeds are disregarded, nor that other crimes shall fail of their just retribution on that awful day. But it is of these works of charity that we are most strongly reminded, because it is these that even good men seem likeliest to forget.

[14] Matt. 25:34-46.

Let us heed, then, our Savior's warning and take pity on the distressed. Let us be good stewards and faithful almoners, spending our goods and labor, with care and gentleness and love, on the helpless members of Christ's family: the great, piteous, suffering multitude of His destitute poor.

*The Apostleship
of Consistency*

*Live out your Faith
in word and deed*

Where is the sincere and thoughtful Catholic who has not strongly wished at times that he could make some converts to the one true Faith? All of us know so deeply, from our everyday experience, the sweetness and the strength, the beauty, tenderness, and power of our holy religion, and the cheer and guidance that it gives us on our way toward Heaven, that we should be dull clods indeed not to desire to share these amazing and neglected treasures with our fellowmen.

It is true, of course, that a sincere and God-fearing non-Catholic may hope to save his soul. True, also, that there is many such a one who puts half-hearted Catholics utterly to shame by the earnestness, uprightness, and goodness of his life. But if such men walk so well in the twilight, how gloriously, we think, they would run onward in the noonday splendor! If they fight so valiantly, nourished with the crumbs that have fallen from the children's table, what heroes they would become if they were fed on the strong Bread of Angels and given to drink of the sweet waters of God's full and satisfying truth? The fervor and earnestness we have noted in so many converts confirms this view and urges us the more to the work of conversion. How ardently they leap forward in the ways of sanctity, when first they feel the mighty aid of the sacraments and of holy Mass! How eagerly they receive the rich teachings of Catholic Tradition and embrace the thousand helps and stays that God's Church alone can give!

He would be an ungenerous and selfish man — or, at least, a very thoughtless one — who had never wished to make a convert to Catholic truth. But when it comes to choosing the means, the average Catholic man or woman may well be perplexed to know just how the good work is to be begun.

"Arguing is no use," they say. "It only makes people stubborn and angry. To explain the truths of Faith is all very good, but how am I to get people to listen, and how am I to answer the awkward questions they will be sure to ask? I cannot write or give lectures or preach sermons. It isn't my business, and, besides, I haven't the talent or the time. So what in the world am I to do?"

This may be all very natural and true, and if these were indeed the only ways of making converts to the Faith, many Catholics might be pardoned for shrinking from the task. Fortunately, these are not the only ways.

There is an argument stronger with most men than any logic — a way of preaching that is open to everyone and to which no living soul can choose but listen: the argument of steadfast good example, of a consistent living up to our Catholic principles and our Catholic beliefs.

We walk about in this world very obscurely, it may be. We do not seem prominent persons in the scheme of things, nor apt to draw men's eyes to look at us. Yet every day of our lives, almost at every hour of our days, at home and in the street, in the busy hours or when we are taking our ease and our pleasure, careless and free and unconscious of the world's remark, we are being watched, studied, thought of, imitated, it may be, by the restless, eager spirits of our fellowmen. What is a man so interested in as in his neighbor? What does he talk of more often? What does he speculate on so eagerly? By what is he so deeply moved as by the sayings and doings, the character and principles of other men?

Blind and deluded though men often are as to their own proper vices and virtues, they have a wonderful shrewdness in searching out and summing up the genuine character of another. It is no use, in the matter of religious principle especially, to try to play the saint and be the sinner. Nothing but sincere and practical fidelity, the pure gold of honesty, seven times tried, will wear well and shine well for long against the rough usage and trying ways of this hurly-burly world.

These are truisms, as we all know; but apply them to yourself, the individual Catholic, moving about in the highways of life and dealing with your fellows. Although they know that you are a Catholic, many of them realize only vaguely what the name implies. But if they recognize in you a man apart from and distinguished above his fellowmen by reason of his honesty, industry, and kindness to his neighbors, by his truth, honor, and good faith, they will grow a bit curious to learn more of what Catholics think and strive for and believe. Your courage, your consistency, and your modest faithfulness to your principles will make you stand out in noble relief against the general carelessness and self-indulgence of the times. They will conceive a huge respect for the Faith that can so lift a man above the common lust and avarice of the world; they will inquire into the Church's teachings and open their hearts to her appeal, and God's grace will have an entrance to win them over to the truth.

And you, sincere, simple, and consistent with your Catholic principles, without any noise of argument or any array of lectures or of books, will truly have converted them; you will have convinced and persuaded them by the most convincing, most persuasive of all arguments: by the solid and practical proof of a life consistent with your holy Faith.

There is another body of non-Catholics who know very well what a Catholic is supposed to profess and practice and believe. They are in need, not of information, but of conviction. They see the beauty of the Faith, but are not quite sure of its truth, and so they waver in that dim borderland which lies between "I doubt" and "I believe."

Your actions, far, far more than your words, have a keen, almost an agonizing interest for such men as these. From the actions of Catholics, they seek to judge, alas, the truth or falsehood of the Catholic Faith. They do not stop to argue that a man may be convinced, but inconsistent, professing high ideals and practicing unworthy ones. They merely say to themselves, "There's So-and-so. He's a Catholic. But see how he acts! In business, he's no better than the rest of us. In his family circle, he's no angel; in his recreations, he's no saint. Yet he's a Catholic. These Catholics do not practice what they preach. No Catholicism for me!"

Live out your Faith in word and deed

Who has hindered his conversion and helped the powers of darkness to keep him from the light? Sad to say, one of the hardest to answer of all arguments against the Faith is the evil behavior of men who profess to believe.

Or, again, more happily, we may hear some non-Catholic remark, "There is So-and-so — a clean, upright, noble fellow if there ever was one. He seems to have some secret that the rest of us lack. Industrious, brisk, businesslike, capable — yes! But he seems all the while to have his heart set on something above and beyond. He believes in a hereafter and lives for it. His family is holy. His home is a sanctuary — bright, clean, cheery, loving — with an atmosphere of peace and joy that are not quite of this world. I'd like to know his secret, and I believe it is his Faith! If it is, then the Catholic religion is the religion for me!" Who has been the chief instrument under God to bring this wavering soul into the light of His Father's house?

Not many weeks ago, at Sunday Mass in one of our great cities, a poor serving-maid was going to Communion. Her faith was pure and deep, and the reverence and love of her soul were strikingly expressed in every look and gesture. How little she dreamed of preaching or giving edification! But one who was not a Catholic, who was hesitating at the very threshold of the Faith, had come to the church that morning and was quietly watching the faithful as they walked up to the Holy Table. "How wonderful the fervor and recollection of that poor girl was!" said she afterward. "You can see how truly she believes that Christ is present in the sacrament."

So it is with us all. Our daily actions blaze out a message and token to the watchful eyes of men.

The Everyday Apostle

If we but knew when we were under observation, we would be doubly careful and consistent then! Well, we are under observation always and everywhere, in the eyes of a critical and watchful age. In the old days, the Church had need of martyrs, which means "witnesses," to give bloody evidence of her truth to a cold, unbelieving world. She has need of martyrs still — not bloody martyrs now, but martyrs to duty, to sincerity, to faith, to the consistent practice of the Christian creed. Who will credit that we believe in the doctrine of the Holy Eucharist, believe that this life-giving Bread is Christ Himself, fearfully humiliated for our love, if we avoid the Tabernacle, where He dwells, until we are driven there on Sunday by the threat of mortal sin? Who will credit us with a faith in the last great judgment if we do not act as though we expect one day to be brought to judgment?

Ah, if we took all this to heart and acted out in every word and deed the Faith that is in us, what noble and effective apostles we would be to bring our friends and fellows into the fold of Christ! Writing is an excellent means to make conversions; kind, tactful conversation is a powerful aid; so is prayer; so is timely comment and explanation. But how the good work done toward converting the world would double and treble — and go on doubling and trebling by leaps and bounds — if only the great body of Catholic men and women would bestir themselves to spread the truth abroad and to shine it, so to speak, in their neighbor's eyes by the strong, direct, appealing, irresistible means of living up steadfastly to the Faith that is in them — by the exercise of the great Apostleship of Consistency!

Biographical Note

☞

Edward F. Garesché, S.J.
(1876-1960)

Born in St. Louis, Missouri, Edward Francis Garesché attended St. Louis University and Washington University and practiced law for two years before entering the Jesuit novitiate in Florrisant, Missouri. He was ordained a priest in 1912.

Fr. Garesché's priesthood was devoted to medical mission work and saw a vast literary output. He wrote seven volumes of poetry, for which he is best known, as well as twenty-four books, ten booklets, and numerous articles on subjects as diverse as prayer, meditation, inspiration, art, history, science, the teachings of the saints, sodality, education, pastoral theology, and nursing. He founded *The Queen's Work*, a magazine of the Sodality of the Blessed Virgin, and edited *Hospital Progress and Medical Mission News*, a publication of the Catholic Medical Mission Board, of which he was president and director.

Fr. Garesché also established the Knights of the Blessed Sacrament in the United States, began a Catholic Young Men's Association, and served as the spiritual director of the International Committee of the Catholic Federation of Nurses and of the Daughters of Mary, Health of the Sick.

The Everyday Apostle

Drawing on his wide-ranging interests and experience and with clear, inspiring words, Fr. Garesché offers his readers practical wisdom on how to find true success in life — that is, the attainment of holiness and happiness through good citizenship, prudent choices, and dutiful service to God and to others.

Sophia Institute Press®